Que® Quick Reference Series

Turbo Pascal® Quick Reference

Michael Yester

Que Corporation
Carmel, Indiana

Library of Congress Catalog Number: 89-60199

ISBN 0-88022-429-0

92 91 90 89   4 3 2

Interpretation of the printing code: the rightmost double-
digit number is the year of the book's printing; the
rightmost single-digit number, the number of the book's
printing. For example, a printing code of 89-4 shows
that the fourth printing of the book occurred in 1989.

Information in this book is based on Turbo Pascal
Version 5. The examples in this book should work with
other releases in which the pertinent features are
available.

Que Quick Reference Series

The *Que Quick Reference Series* is a portable resource
of essential microcomputer knowledge. Whether you are
a new or experienced user, you can rely on the high-
quality information contained in these convenient
guides.

Drawing on the experience of many of Que's best-
selling authors, the *Que Quick Reference Series* helps
you easily access important program information. Now
it's easy to look up programming information for assembly language, C, DOS and BIOS functions, QuickBA-
SIC 4, and Turbo Pascal as well as frequently used
commands and functions for 1-2-3, WordPerfect 5, MS-
DOS, dBASE IV, and AutoCAD.

Use the *Que Quick Reference Series* as a compact
alternative to confusing and complicated traditional
documentation.

The *Que Quick Reference Series* also includes these
titles:

Assembly Language Quick Reference
AutoCAD Quick Reference
DOS and BIOS Functions Quick Reference
C Quick Reference
QuickBASIC Quick Reference
1-2-3 Quick Reference
dBASE IV Quick Reference
Hard Disk Quick Reference
MS-DOS Quick Reference
WordPerfect Quick Reference

Publishing Manager
Allen L. Wyatt, Sr.

Product Development Specialist
Bill Nolan

Senior Editor
Gregory Croy

Technical Editor
Chris Land

Editorial Assistant
Ann K. Taylor

Trademark Acknowledgments

Que Corporation has made every effort to supply trademark information about company names, products, and services mentioned in this book. Trademarks indicated below were derived from various sources. Que Corporation cannot attest to the accuracy of this information.

IBM and IBM 8514/A are registered trademarks of International Business Machines Corporation.

Turbo Pascal is a registered trademark of Borland International, Inc.

Table of Contents

Using Turbo Pascal's Integrated Development Environment

Start Turbo Pascal from the DOS prompt by typing **TURBO** and pressing the Enter key. The first screen that appears contains product version information. Press any key to begin.

You are now inside the Turbo Pascal *integrated development environment* (IDE). Within the IDE, you can load, enter, edit, save, compile, debug, and run Turbo Pascal programs. You can invoke these features through special combinations of keystrokes or by executing the commands within the pull-down menus that appear across the top of the screen.

Any time you want, you can leave the IDE and return to DOS by pressing Alt-X.

Turbo Pascal's Main Menu Line

To select a menu, press the first letter of the menu's name or use the right- and left-arrow keys to move to the desired menu and then press the Enter key. Press Esc to leave a menu.

To select a command from a menu, press the high-lighted letter or use the up- and down-arrow keys to move to the desired command and then press Enter. Press Esc to cancel a command before you execute it.

Press F10 to toggle between the menu line and the Edit window.

From the Edit window, you can move to a specific menu by holding down the Alt key and entering the first letter of the menu's name. For example, Alt-F takes you directly to the File menu.

The most commonly used commands can also be invoked with *hot keys*—special combinations of keystrokes that allow you to bypass the menu selection

process and execute a command directly. For example,
F2 saves the file in the editor.

The following sections describe the menus and summa-
rize their individual commands. A hot key, if available,
is shown in parentheses following the command name.

The File Menu (Alt-F)

The File menu allows you to load, save, and create
program files, to select directories, and—with the *OS
Shell* option—to temporarily suspend the execution of
the compiler and return to the operating system. The File
menu's commands include the following:

Load (F3)

Loads a file from disk. You may specify a file name
either by typing or selecting it.

Pick (Alt-F3)

Allows you to select and load a file from among the
eight most recently edited files.

New

Erases the program currently in the editor and changes
the default file name to NONAME.PAS. Use this
command when you want to begin a new program.

Save (F2)

Saves the file in the editor to disk using the current
program name.

Write To

Saves the file in the editor to disk after prompting for a
new program name. Use this command when you want
to change the name of the file.

Directory

Displays the contents of the current directory.

Change Dir

Displays the complete path of the current directory and allows you to select a new default directory.

OS Shell

Suspends Turbo Pascal and takes you to DOS in the currently active directory. To return to Turbo Pascal, type **EXIT** at the DOS prompt.

Quit (Alt-X)

Quits Turbo Pascal and takes you to DOS in the currently active directory.

The Edit Command (Alt-E)

The **Edit** command takes you to the main part of the screen, where you can use the built-in editor.

The Run Menu (Alt-R)

The Run menu controls program execution. The Run menu's commands include the following:

Run (Ctrl-F9)

Runs the program currently in the editor. If necessary, Turbo will automatically compile the program before the execution occurs.

Program Reset (Ctrl-F2)

Terminates the current debugging session and resets the program.

Go To Cursor (F4)

Executes all program statements up to the line containing the cursor. The program is compiled if necessary.

Trace Into (F7)

Executes the next program statement. If the next statement is a procedure or function call, then the procedure or function is also executed one line at a time.

Step Over (F8)

Executes the next program statement. If the next statement is a procedure or function call, then the procedure or function is executed in a single step.

User Screen (Alt-F5)

Displays the program output screen.

The Compile Menu (Alt-C)

The Compile menu controls the compilation of programs and units. The Compile menu's commands include the following:

Compile (Alt-F9)

Compiles the program currently in the editor and displays the results in a special window.

Make (F9)

Checks the current source text plus any units used by the current source text. Units are recompiled if their source has been changed since the last compilation, then the source text is compiled.

Build

Recompiles any units used by the current source text and then compiles the current source text itself.

Destination
Selects between compiling the current source text to memory (the default) or to disk.

Find Error
Finds the program line corresponding to a specific segment:offset memory address.

Primary File
Specifies the primary .PAS file for use by the **Make** and **Build** commands.

Get Info
Displays information about the file in the editor.

The Options Menu (Alt-O)

The Options menu controls the system-wide defaults. The Options menu's commands include the following:

Compiler
Specifies the default compiler options, which include:

Compiler Option	Directive	Default
Range Checking	$R	Off
Stack Checking	$S	On
I/O Checking	$I	On
Force Far Calls	$F	Off
Overlays Allowed	$O	Off
Align Data	$A	Word
Var-String Checking	$V	Strict
Boolean Evaluation	$B	Short Circuit
Numeric Processing	$N	Software
Emulation	$E	On
Debug Information	$D	On
Local Symbols	$L	On
Conditional Defines	$DEFINE	No defaults
Memory Sizes	$M	16384, 0, 655360

Linker

Specifies the default linker options pertaining to the
.MAP file and link buffer.

Environment

Specifies the default environment options.

Directories

Specifies the directories the compiler should use when
searching for configuration, include, unit, object, and
pick files and the directories where compiled .EXE and
.TPU files should be stored.

Parameters

Specifies the default command-line parameters.

Save Options

Saves all *Compiler*, *Environment*, and *Directories*
options in a configuration file with a default name of
TURBO.TP.

Retrieve Options

Loads and sets all *Compiler*, *Environment*, and *Directories* options saved with the **Save Options** command.
The default configuration file name is TURBO.TP.

The Debug Menu (Alt-D)

The Debug menu contains many of the commands that
control the use of the built-in debugger. The Debug
menu's commands include the following:

Evaluate (Ctrl-F4)

During a debugging session, allows you to evaluate
expressions and change the value of any variable.

Call Stack (Ctrl-F3)

During a debugging session, displays the list—in sequence—of the currently executing procedure and function calls together with their parameters.

Find Procedure

Moves the cursor to the first line of a specified procedure or function. The program must have already been compiled in order for this command to be available.

Integrated Debugging

Controls whether Turbo Pascal's integrated debugger is enabled. The default setting is *On*.

Stand-Alone Debugging

Specifies whether the compiler is to produce the necessary tables that support Borland's stand-alone Turbo Debugger product. The default setting is *Off*. The program must be compiled to disk.

Display Swapping

During a debugging session, controls swapping of the display between the execution window and the integrated environment.

Refresh Display

During a debugging session, restores the screen after your program—executed while the Display Swapping switch was set to *None*—overwrites the display.

The Break/Watch Menu (Alt-B)

The Break/Watch menu allows you to control execution of your program and to view variables. The Break/Watch menu's commands include the following:

Add Watch (Ctrl-F7)

Adds a variable or an expression to the top of the Watch window.

Delete Watch

Deletes the current item from the Watch window. A dot identifies the current Watch item.

Edit Watch

Edits the current watch expression.

Remove All Watches

Clears all items from the Watch window.

Toggle Breakpoint (Ctrl-F8)

Sets a breakpoint at the line containing the cursor. If the line is already a breakpoint, the breakpoint is cleared.

Clear All Breakpoints

Clears all breakpoints.

View Next Breakpoint

Moves the cursor to the next breakpoint or back to the first breakpoint if no breakpoints remain in the program.

On-Line Help Information

You can obtain on-line help any time you need it. Press F1 to display the help window. Press F1 again to display the help index. Position the cursor over the desired topic and press the Enter key. You can obtain *context-sensitive* help information about any standard unit, procedure, function, constant, type, or variable. Position the cursor over the item and press Ctrl-F1.

To redisplay the previous help window, press Alt-F1. Press Esc to exit the help window.

Turbo Pascal Hot Keys

The most commonly used Turbo Pascal menu commands can be executed with the following hot keys.

Key	Action
F1	Displays Help information
F2	The File menu **Save** command
F3	The File menu **Load** command
F4	The Run menu **Go to Cursor** command
F5	Zooms/unzooms the active window
F6	Changes the active window
F7	The Run menu **Trace Into** command
F8	The Run menu **Step Over** command
F9	The Compile menu **Make** command
F10	Switches between the main menu and the active window
Alt-F1	Redisplays the last Help screen
Alt-F3	The File menu **Pick** command
Alt-F5	The Run menu **User Screen** command
Alt-F6	Switches between the Watch and Execution menus
Alt-F9	The Compile menu **Compile** command
Alt-B	Takes you to the Break/Watch menu
Alt-C	Takes you to the Compile menu
Alt-D	Takes you to the Debug menu
Alt-E	Takes you to the editor
Alt-F	Takes you to the File menu
Alt-O	Takes you to the Options menu
Alt-R	Takes you to the Run menu
Alt-X	The File menu **Quit** command
Ctrl-F1	Displays language help within the editor
Ctrl-F2	The Run menu **Program Reset** command
Ctrl-F3	The Debug menu **Call Stack** command
Ctrl-F4	The Debug menu **Evaluate** command
Ctrl-F7	The Break/Watch menu **Add Watch** command
Ctrl-F8	The Break/Watch menu **Toggle Breakpoint** command
Ctrl-F9	The Run menu **Run** command
Shift-F10	Displays the version screen

Using the Turbo Pascal Editor

Turbo Pascal's editor allows you to enter and edit source text using commands similar to those in WordStar.

Cursor Movement

The following commands move the cursor through the source text without modifying the file.

Move one line down	Ctrl-X or ↓
Move one position left	Ctrl-S or ←
Move one position right	Ctrl-D or →
Move one line up	Ctrl-E or ↑
Move to start of word to left	Ctrl-A or Ctrl- ←
Move to start of word to right	Ctrl-F or Ctrl- →
Scrolls text down one line	Ctrl-Z
Scrolls text up one line	Ctrl-W
Scrolls text down one page	Ctrl-C or PgDn
Scrolls text up one page	Ctrl-R or PgUp
Move to beginning of line	Ctrl-QS or Home
Move to end of line	Ctrl-QD or End
Move to top of window	Ctrl-QE or Ctrl-Home
Move to bottom of window	Ctrl-QX or Ctrl-End
Move to beginning of program	Ctrl-QR or Ctrl-PgUp
Move to end of program	Ctrl-QC or Ctrl-PgDn
Move to beginning of block	Ctrl-QB
Move to end of block	Ctrl-QK
Return to previous position	Ctrl-QP
Move to last error position	Ctrl-QW

Character Insertion and Deletion

The following commands specify how characters can be inserted and deleted.

Delete character under cursor	Ctrl-G or Del
Delete character left of cursor	Ctrl-H or Backspace
Delete the entire line	Ctrl-Y
Delete from cursor to end of line	Ctrl-QY
Delete word to right of cursor	Ctrl-T
Insert a new line	Ctrl-N
Toggle the insert mode	Ctrl-V or Ins

Block Commands

The following commands select and manage blocks of source text.

Mark beginning of block	Ctrl-KB or F7
Mark end of block	Ctrl-KK or F8
Mark a single word	Ctrl-KT
Print block	Ctrl-KP
Copy block	Ctrl-KC
Delete block	Ctrl-KY
Hide/Display block	Ctrl-KH
Move block	Ctrl-KV
Read block from disk	Ctrl-KR
Write block to disk	Ctrl-KW
Indent block	Ctrl-KI
Unindent block	Ctrl-KU

Miscellaneous Commands

The following commands perform the remaining text management functions.

Abort current operation	Ctrl-U
Autoindent on/off	Ctrl-OI or Ctrl-QI
Control char prefix	Ctrl-P
Exit editor, no save	Ctrl-KD or Ctrl-KQ
Find and replace	Ctrl-QA
Find string	Ctrl-QF

Go to error position	Ctrl-QW
Insert directives	Ctrl-OO
Invoke main menu	F10
Language help	Ctrl-F1
Load file	F3
Move to marker n (n = 0 to 3)	Ctrl-Qn
Optimal fill on/off	Ctrl-OF
Pair braces backward	Ctrl-Q]
Pair braces forward	Ctrl-Q[
Repeat last find	Ctrl-L
Restore line	Ctrl-QL
Save file	Ctrl-KS or F2
Set marker n (n = 0 to 3)	Ctrl-Kn
Tab	Ctrl-I or Tab
Tab mode toggle	Ctrl-OT or Ctrl-QT
Unindent on/off	Ctrl-OU

Debugging Your Program

To debug a program, execute it up to the point at which the problem appears. You can then examine the contents of variables, and, if necessary, you can even change their values. Both the {$D} and the {$L} options must be enabled.

Move to a Specific Point in the Program

To execute all program statements up to (but not including) the questionable part of the program, position the cursor on the first program statement you want to examine and execute the Run menu's **Go to Cursor** command (F4). If necessary, Turbo will automatically compile the program before the execution occurs. If you've changed the program since its last compilation, Turbo will ask you if it should recompile the code before it proceeds.

Adding a Watch Variable

Keeping track of a variable throughout the execution of a program is called *watching*. Specifying which variable to track is called *adding a watch*. Use the Break/Watch menu's **Add Watch** command (Ctrl-F7) to add a variable or an expression to the Watch window.

You can switch between the editor and the Watch window by pressing the F6 key. When the Watch window is active, use the Ins key to add more items.

Editing a Watch Variable

You can *modify* the expression being watched without restarting the program. Use the Break/Watch menu's **Edit Watch** command to copy the current watch expression to a special *Edit Watch* window and use the editing keys to modify the expression. Press Enter to install the change, or Esc to cancel it.

To change the current Watch item, switch to the Watch window by pressing F6, and use the cursor control keys to position the cursor over the item you want. You can select the current item for editing more easily by simply pressing the Enter key. Press F6 once again to return to the editor.

Establishing a Breakpoint

Program execution is temporarily suspended at user-defined *breakpoints*. The Break/Watch menu's **Toggle Breakpoint** command (Ctrl-F8) selects the line containing the cursor as a breakpoint.

Executing the Program

There are three commands you can use to execute statements during a debugging session.

The Run menu's **Run** command (Ctrl-F9) causes program execution to resume from the point at which it was last interrupted. Execution halts when the program terminates when you press Ctrl-Break, or the next break-point is encountered.

The Run menu's **Trace Into** command (F7) executes only the *next* program statement. If the statement is a procedure or function call, then the procedure or function itself is also executed a line at a time. If the next executable line happens to reside in another unit or in an include file, the debugger will automatically load that file before proceeding.

The Run menu's **Step Over** command (F8) is similar to the **Trace Into** command, except that if the next line is a procedure or function call, then the procedure or function is executed in a *single* step.

Deleting a Watch Variable

The Break/Watch menu's **Delete Watch** command deletes the current watch item. To change the current watch item, switch to the Watch window by pressing the F6 key, and use the cursor control keys to make another selection. Press F6 once again to return to the editor.

Within the Watch window itself, you can delete an item by simply using the Del key.

Terminating the Debugging Session

The Run menu's **Program Reset** command (Ctrl-F2) terminates the current debugging run. Any dynamic memory allocated by the program is released. Any open files are closed. Typed constants are reset, but any variables are left untouched. The next line to be executed will be the first executable line of the program.

Programming Essentials

Turbo Pascal source text consists of series of characters arranged to produce a meaningful program.

Characters

A character is any one of the 256 standard or extended ASCII characters. A character can be written either by typing its "normal" symbol (for example the letter *A*) or by preceding the ASCII value (an integer in the range 0 through 255) with the # symbol. Hence, the letter *A* can also be written as #65.

Unprintable characters are always written with the # symbol. For example, the character pair #7 represents the single character corresponding to the bell sound.

Identifiers

An identifier can consist of any number of continuous letters, digits, and underscores, but the first character must be a letter or an underscore. Upper- and lowercase letters are considered identical. Identifiers can be any length, but only the first 63 characters are significant.

Reserved Words

Following is a list of all reserved words in Turbo Pascal. A reserved word cannot be used as the identifier of any program, constant, type, label, variable, procedure, or function.

absolute	if	record
and	implemen-	repeat
array	tation	set
begin	in	shl
case	inline	shr
const	interface	string
div	interrupt	then
do	label	to
downto	mod	type
else	nil	unit
end	not	until
external	of	uses
file	or	var
for	packed	while
forward	procedure	with
function	program	xor
goto		

Strings

A *string* is a sequence of zero or more ASCII characters contained in a single program line and enclosed in apostrophes (single quotation marks). A string with no characters between the apostrophes is called a *null* string. If an apostrophe is desired *within* a string, it must be written twice.

If a control character is included in a string, it must be placed outside any apostrophes; if the control character is in the middle of a string, the string must be temporarily closed and then reopened.

Numbers

Numbers consist of any valid combination of digits, plus and minus signs, and decimal points. Commas may not be used. Numbers can be broadly grouped as *real* or *integer*. A real number is one that contains a decimal point; an integer doesn't. Any decimal point used in a real number must be preceded by a digit. For example, the number .6 must be written as 0.6.

Real numbers may be written in scientific notation using the letter "E" or "e" (8.3E-4). Hexadecimal numbers are written with a leading dollar sign ($10, $FF, or $a0).

Symbols

The following symbols have special meanings:

=	Used in type and constant declaration
( )	Grouping symbols for complex expressions; also used for subroutine headings and calls and for declaring enumeration types
$	When used before a number, indicates that the number is hexadecimal
#	When used before a number, indicates that the number is an ASCII value code

;	Used to separate statements and terminate declarations
:=	Assignment
:	Used in variable declarations, labels, case statements, function headings, and in formatting output
'	(single quotation mark) Used with quoted and constant strings
.	(period) Used to terminate programs and units and to access the fields of a record
,	(comma) Used to separate identifiers and parameters
..	(double period) Subrange; also used in array subscript declaration
^	Denotes a pointer
(. .) or [ ]	Brackets for arrays or sets
(* *) or { }	Comment delimiters

The following are used as arithmetic operators.

*	Multiplication/set intersection
+	Addition/concatenation/set union
-	Subtraction/set difference/unary negate
/	Real division
<	Less than
<=	Less than or equal to/set inclusion
<>	Not equal to
=	Equal to
>	Greater than
>=	Greater than or equal to/set inclusion
@	Address

All other symbols are *undefined* and can only appear within a string.

Tokens and Separators

Each sequence of characters having a common meaning is called a *token*. Two adjacent tokens must be divided by at least one *separator*. The space character and *all* control characters (ASCII 0 through 32) are separators.

Comments

The characters { and } or (* and *) *comment*—a special form of separator that defines an area of text that's completely ignored by the compiler. Comments are principally used for program documentation:

```
(* This is a comment *)
```

The compiler treats the entire comment as a single space. A comment can appear anywhere in the program. Everything inside a comment is ignored unless a dollar sign ($) is placed in its first position. The $ indicates that the comment is a compiler *directive*.

Program Data

All data in Turbo Pascal must be declared before it can be used. The individual declarations of labels, constants, types, and variables can occur in any sequence.

Data Declarations

Label Declarations

Pascal uses a *label* to mark a location within a block of program code.

Labels are declared with the reserved word `label` followed by the desired identifiers. In standard Pascal, each identifier may consist of a whole number from 0 to 9999. Turbo Pascal also allows labels to be normal alphanumeric identifier names. If several labels are declared, each pair must be separated with a comma. The final label must be followed by a semicolon.

When a label is used in the program, it must be the first identifier on the line. Each label must be immediately followed by a colon (:).

Constant Definitions

The constant declaration section begins with the reserved word `const`. Each individual constant is declared as an identifier, followed by an equal sign (=), followed by the value to be assigned to the identifier, and finally followed by a semicolon.

Examples of constant declarations are as follows:

```
const
    TopLine     = 6;
```

Constant Expressions

Constant expressions can be used in the place of a single constant. Anything appearing in a constant expression must be completely defined by the time the expression is encountered. Consequently, expressions can't contain references to variables, typed constants, function calls, or the address operator (@). However, the following standard functions may be used:

```
Abs   Chr Hi     Length Lo    Odd   Ord
Pred  Ptr Round  SizeOf Succ  Swap  Trunc
```

Examples are:

```
const
    PageLength  = BottomLine - TopLine + 1;
    FormFeed    = Chr(12);
```

Typed Constants

Turbo Pascal supports the use of *typed constants*, which enable you to assign not only an initial value to a variable, but a type as well.

Although typed constants are declared within the constant section, they are really variables.

Each typed constant is written in the form: identifier, colon (:), type, equal sign (=), and initial value:

```
const
    NumberOfFlights : integer = 4;
```

Any valid type may be used, including numbers, strings, arrays, records, and sets.

Type Definitions

Type is the property of a Pascal variable that defines the size of the storage it requires, the range of values it can be assigned, and the operators which can act on it.

A type declaration section begins with the reserved word `type`. Each individual type is written in the form of an identifier, followed by an equal sign (=), followed by a description of the type and a semicolon.

```
Type
   Inventory = record
                    Item : string[ 30 ]
                    Cost : real;
               end;
```

Variable Declarations

A variable declaration section begins with the reserved word `var`. Each variable is written in the form of an identifier followed by a colon, the variable type, and a semicolon. A variable may be of any standard or user-defined type.

```
var
    i             : byte;
    ProductKey    : string[ 12 ];
```

Data Types

Turbo Pascal provides several predefined data types. In addition, it allows you to create your own data types.

Integers

Five data types store integers:

Type	Size	Ranges of Allowed Values
Byte	1 byte	0..255
ShortInt	1 byte	-128..+127
Integer	2 bytes	-32,768..+32,767
Word	2 bytes	0..65,535
LongInt	4 bytes	-2,147,483,648..+2,147,483,647

Reals

Five data types store real numbers:

Type	Size	Value Ranges	Signif. Digits
Real	6 bytes	$2.9 \times 10^{-39} .. 1.7 \times 10^{38}$	11-12
Single	4 bytes	$1.5 \times 10^{-45} .. 3.4 \times 10^{38}$	7-8
Double	8 bytes	$5.0 \times 10^{-324} .. 1.7 \times 10^{308}$	15-16
Extended	10 bytes	$3.4 \times 10^{-4932} .. 1.1 \times 10^{4932}$	19-20
Comp	8 bytes	$-2^{63}+1 .. 2^{63}-1$	19-20

The `single`, `double`, `extended`, and `comp` data types are supported either with software emulation (with the `{$E+}` compiler directive) or with an 8087-family coprocessor (with the `{$N+}` compiler directive).

Booleans

Boolean variables can either be `True` or `False`.

Characters

Three data types handle individual bytes: `Char`, `Byte`, and `ShortInt`. `Byte` and `ShortInt` store type is used. When a byte is used to represent one of the 256 extended ASCII characters, the `Char` type is used.

Strings

A *string* type consists of a series of ASCII characters. A string is declared with the following format:

```
var
    StrVar : string[ StringSize ];
```

The maximum `StringSize` is 255 characters. If the reserved word `string` appears *without* a size indicator, then 255 is used as the default. The individual characters can be accessed with subscripts; for example, `Name[5]` references the fifth character of the `Name` string.

Enumerated Types

The *enumerated* type is a list of identifiers enclosed in parentheses. Every identifier in the list must be individually enumerated.

```
type
   Crayons = ( Red, Orange,, Green, Blue );
var
   Color : Crayons;
```

The variable `Color` can take on any of the identifiers defined by `Crayons`.

Subrange Types

The *subrange* is a subset of a previously defined type, called the *host* type. A subrange of real numbers isn't allowed. The range must be continuous. You define it by declaring the upper and lower bounds with two periods (. .) separating them:

```
var
   WorkingAge : 18..65;
```

If the Range-Checking option {$R+} is enabled, the compiler ensures that any variable of a subrange type remains within the specified range.

Sets

A *set* is a finite collection of elements that share the same previously defined type, called the *base* type. A set variable is declared as:

```
var
   Bunch : set of BaseType;
```

The maximum number of elements in a set is 256, and the upper and lower bounds of the base type must have ordinal values that are within the range 0 through 255. Consequently, the base type of a set can't be a `ShortInt`, `Integer`, `LongInt`, or `Word`.

Examples of sets are as follows:

```
type
   Days = ( Sun, Mon, Tue, Wed, Thu,
            Fri, Sat );
var
   WorkDays : set of Days;
```

When you assign values to a set type, such as `Work-Days`, you do it by placing the identifiers within brackets, as follows:

```
WorkDays := [ Mon, Tue, Wed, Thu, Fri ];
```

Pointers

Pointer variables contain the memory *address* of a data structure rather than the data structure itself. A pointer variable can be defined in either of the following ways:

```
var
   Var1 : ^BaseType;
   Var2 : pointer;
```

Var1 is a pointer to a variable of type BaseType. Var1 can only be used to point to BaseType variables. Var2 is a general pointer and can be used to point to a variable of any type.

The pointer can be defined as something declared later in the same section:

```
type
   DataArrow = ^DataStuff;
   DataStuff = record
                   Info1   : real;
                   Info2   : integer;
                   DataPtr : DataArrow;
               end;
```

Arrays

An *array* is a fixed number of variables that all have the same type. Each element of the array can be accessed by specifying its *index*.

An array type is declared as follows:

```
var
   ArrayName : array [ IndexType ]
               of ArrayType;
```

IndexType is a subrange that specifies the array's dimensions. Any ordinal subrange is allowed, with the exception of LongInt. ArrayType may be any standard or user-defined data type. ArrayType may even be another array, in which case the declaration would appear as follows:

```
var
   Array1 : array [ 1..5 ]
          of array [ 1..10 ] of integer;
```

Multi-dimensional arrays can also be defined in the
following manner:

```
var
   Array2 : array [ 1..5, 1..10 ]
          of integer;
```

Records

A *record* is a data type that consists of any combination
of *fields*, each of which is a variable of any data type.
An example of a record definition is as follows:

```
type
   Passenger = record
                  Name     : string;
                  FlightNum : word;
               end;
```

Each field can be individually accessed in the form

```
RecordIdentifier.FieldName
```

For example, if Traveler is defined as type Passen-
ger, then the fields in Traveler can be accessed as
Traveler.Name and Traveler.FlightNum.

Variant Records

A variant record is defined by first listing all common
fields, then by using a case statement to identify the
individual groups, or variants. Each variant may be a
different length, but must be referenced with an ordinal
constant. For example:

```
type
   Accum = record
             case integer of
                1 : ( AX     : word );
                2 : ( AL, AH : byte );
           end;
var
   Settings : Accum;
```

Frequently, you need to keep track of which variant is in
use. This can be accomplished by an extra field, called a

tag field, used to identify the active variant.

```
type
   Flight  = ( Domestic, Overseas );
   PassRec = record
      Name      : string;
      FlightNum : word;
      case Dest : Flight of
         Domestic : ( City, State : string );
         Overseas : ( Tax : real;
                         Country : string );
      end;
var
   Traveler : PassRec;
```

Dest is the tag field and is actually stored as a separate field within the PassRec record. Its value can be either Domestic or Overseas.

Files

A *file* is a sequence of components of the same type. A component may be a standard type, such as Byte or Word, or it may be a user-defined type such as a record. There may be any number of components, but they may only be accessed one at a time. There are three types of files, named for the syntax of their declarations: *text*, *typed*, and *untyped*.

```
var
   FileName1 : file of DataRec; { Typed }
   FileName2 : file;            { Untyped }
   FileName3 : Text;            { Text }
```

A *typed file* contains *only* data of the one particular type named in the declaration. An *untyped file* is completely unstructured. It may contain any data in any format in any length. A *text file* contains lines of characters (that is, data of type char) terminated by a carriage return (#13) and, usually, a line feed (#10) as well. Lines may vary in length. Note that a text file is *not* the same as a file of type char.

Procedure Types

Turbo Pascal allows you to assign a procedure or function to a variable declared as a *procedure type*.

This enables a procedure or function to be treated just like an ordinary data object.

A procedure type declaration is declared just like an ordinary procedure or function header but without the subroutine name.

Sample procedure type declarations are as follows:

```
type
    Binary  = function (B1,B2 : word) : word;
    ProcHold = procedure;
```

Any procedure or function having a *similar combination* of parameters and types defined in its header may be assigned to any variable defined as a compatible type. Any subroutine you want to assign a procedure-type variable must be compiled with the *{$F+} Force Far Calls* option enabled.

Program Control Statements

Program code is defined by executable statements that specify the actions to be taken by the program. Statements are the active, data movement and manipulation commands. From their content, the compiler determines the machine instructions to be generated.

Assignment

An *assignment* statement replaces the current value of a variable with a new value. The new value can either be explicitly defined, as in

```
Quantity := 45;                { Number }
```

or it can be stated as an expression, which may contain functions, from which the value can be derived, as in

```
X := 45 div 9;        { Expression }
```

Case

A *case* statement allows you to select one out of several sets of actions depending on the result of a single test. The expression to be tested is called the *selector*, and each option is called a *case constant*. If the selector doesn't match any of the case constants, the statement identified with the word `else` will be executed. If the selector doesn't match any of the case constants, but no `else` clause is present, then control simply passes to the first statement following the `case` statement.

The selector expression should evaluate to an ordinal value within the range -32,768 through +32,767. Hence, strings, real numbers, and the integer types `longint` and `word` can't be used as selectors.

`Case` statements can be demonstrated with the following examples:

```
case MenuOption1 of
   1 : DoTask1;
   2 : DoTask2;
   3 : case MenuOption2 of
       1 : DoTask3A;
       2 : DoTask3B;
       end;
   4 : DoTask4;
else  DemandRetype;
end;
```

For..To/DownTo..Do

The *for loop* executes a statement repeatedly, while a sequence of values is assigned to a control variable. The reserved word `to` indicates an increase in the control variable, and `downto` indicates a decrease:

```
for i := 'a' to 'z' do
   write( i );      { Outputs the alphabet }
for i := 'z' downto 'a' do
   write( i );      { Reverses the alphabet }
```

Goto

The goto statement transfers the program flow to the
first statement following a label. For example:

```
goto LabeledLine;
```

causes a jump to the statement immediately following
the referenced label, which must be located within the
same block as the goto itself.

If..Then..Else

The if statement tests a condition; *if* the condition is
True, *then* a statement is executed. For example:

```
if RecordCount > 100 then
    Write( 'It''s time to save your file!' );
```

The option else specifies the alternate action:

```
if FileExists then
    OpenTheFile
else
    CreateTheFile;
```

If the statements being executed consist of other if
statements, then the compiler assumes that each else
is associated with the last unmatched if.

Repeat..Until

The repeat loop repeats a series of statements one or
more times until a specified condition becomes True.

```
repeat
    write( 'Continue (Y/N)?: ' );
    readln( Answer );
until (Answer = 'Y') or (Answer = 'N');
```

While..Do

The `while` loop repeats a series of statements until a
condition becomes `False`:

```
Total := 0;
readln( Entry );
while Entry <> 0 do
   begin
      Total := Total + Entry;
      readln( Entry );
   end;
writeln( 'The total is ', Total );
```

With

A `with` statement allows you to reference the fields of
a record without specifying the record name with each
use. For example, given the following declarations:

```
type FlightInfo = record
                     Name   : string;
                     Flight : word;
                  end;
var Passenger : FlightInfo;
```

then the following sets of code are identical:

```
begin
   Passenger.Name   := 'Smith';
   Passenger.Flight := 703;
end;
```

and

```
with Passenger do
   begin
      Name   := 'Smith';
      Flight := 703;
   end;
```

Compound Statements

A *compound* statement consists of the reserved words
begin and end, between which any number of other
valid statements may be located. As far as the compiler
is concerned, the begin and end pair define a single
statement, as shown in the following example:

```
if QuantitySold > 1000 then
    begin
        writeln( 'Great job!' );
        Commission := QuantitySold * 5.00;
    end
else
    begin
        writeln( 'You missed your quota.' );
        Commission := 0;
    end;
```

Operators

Turbo has operators to perform all the customary
arithmetic and logical operations.

Operator Precedence

The order of operator precedence is given in the following table. Unless otherwise grouped by parentheses, all
operators on the same line have equal precedence and
are evaluated in the order they are written.

Precedence	Operators
1 (High)	@ NOT unary +,-
2	* / DIV MOD AND SHL SHR
3	binary +,- OR XOR
4 (Low)	= <> < > <= >= IN

Arithmetic Operators

The addition, subtraction, multiplication, and division
operators perform just as their names imply. The only
exception is that the / operator can only be used for real
division; the DIV operator must be used for integer
division.

Operator	Syntax	Meaning
+	+expr	Positive (unary)
+	expr1 + expr2	Addition (binary)
-	-expr	Negative (unary)
-	expr1 - expr2	Subtraction (binary)
*	expr1 * expr2	Multiplication
/	expr1 / expr2	Real division
DIV	expr1 DIV expr2	Integer division
MOD	expr1 MOD expr2	Remainder (modulus)

Shift Operators

The SHL (shift bits left) and SHR (shift bits right) operators are used to slide the bits in an integer to the left and right, respectively. For example

```
VarName SHL 2
```

shifts all bits in the variable VarName two places to the left.

Bits shifted off either end of the expression are lost. Bits on the right for SHL and on the left for SHR are zero-filled as their original contents are moved over.

Boolean Operators

Boolean operators perform Boolean manipulations that use entire operands. AND compares two operands and returns True only if both operands are True. OR compares two operands and returns True if either operand is True. XOR compares two operands and returns True only if the operands are different. NOT returns the opposite state of an operand.

Operator	Syntax	Meaning
NOT	NOT expr	Complement
AND	expr1 AND expr2	AND
OR	expr1 OR expr2	Inclusive OR
XOR	expr1 XOR expr2	Exclusive OR

Logical Operators

Logical operators perform Boolean comparisons on individual bits, setting the resulting bits based upon the comparison. AND sets the result if both bits are set. OR sets the result if either bit is set. XOR sets the result if the bits are different. NOT reverses the bits.

Relational Operators

Relational operators compare two expressions and return True if the condition specified by the operator is satisfied, or False if it is not. The operators and their return values are as follows:

Oper	*Syntax*	*Returns "True" if:*
=	expr1 = expr2	Expressions are equal
<>	expr1 <> expr2	Expressions are not equal
<	expr1 < expr2	Expr1 is less than expr2
<=	expr1 <= expr2	Expr1 is less than or equal to expr2
>	expr1 > expr2	Expr1 is greater than expr2
>=	expr1 >= expr2	Expr1 is greater than or equal to expr2

Relational tests are used wherever Boolean expressions are allowed. This includes if..then, repeat.. until, and while...do, statements.

Two strings are compared lexicographically, using the same rules as those that sequence dictionary entries. Strings are sorted according to ASCII value of each character. For purposes of comparison, an operand of type char is treated as a string of length one.

Relational Set Operators

The *relational set operators* test either for equality or *inclusion*.

Oper	*Syntax*	*Returns "True" if:*
=	Set1 = Set2	Set1 equals Set2.
<>	Set1 <> Set2	One of the sets contains at least one element that isn't in the other set.
<=	Set1 <= Set2	Every element in Set1 is also in Set2.

`<`	`Set1 < Set2`	Every element in `Set1` is in `Set2`, and `Set2` contains at least one other element not in `Set1`.
`>=`	`Set1 >= Set2`	Every element in `Set2` is also in `Set1`.
`>`	`Set1 > Set2`	Every element in `Set2` is in `Set1`, and `Set1` contains at least one other element not in `Set2`.
`IN`	`elem IN Set1`	Element "elem" is found in `Set1`.

Set Membership Operators

Three main operations can be performed on the elements of sets: union, difference, and intersection. The results of these operations conform to the ordinary rules of logic.

The union operator (+) produces a set which contains one of every element found in either operand. For example, the union

[1, 2, 3, 4, 5] + [3, 4, 5, 6, 7]

produces the set

[1, 2, 3, 4, 5, 6, 7]

The difference operator (-) produces a set which contains all elements of the first set that are *not* found in the second set. For example,

[1, 2, 3, 4, 5] - [3, 4, 5, 6, 7]

produces the set

[1, 2]

The intersection operator (*) returns a set containing elements common to *both* set operands. For example,

[1, 2, 3, 4, 5] * [3, 4, 5, 6, 7]

produces the set

[3, 4, 5]

Address Operator

The *address* operator @ returns the address of any variable, procedure, or function. It produces the same result as the old Addr function. The @ operator returns a value that is compatible with all pointer types.

String Operator

Using + on operands of string or char types returns a single string which is the concatenation of the two operands. The resulting string cannot exceed 255 characters; any excess characters are truncated on the right. The new string consists of only the active portions of the operands.

Using Procedures and Functions

A procedure is a subroutine that results in series of actions directed toward a single purpose. A function is a subroutine designed to return a value; accordingly, functions are called only within expressions.

Parameter Passing

The parameters in a procedure or function heading are called *formal* parameters. When the subroutine is called, *actual* parameters are used. The types of the actual and formal parameters must be compatible. Turbo Pascal provides three ways to specify a parameter.

1. A parameter *not* preceded by the reserved word var, but followed by a specific type, is called a *value parameter*.

2. A parameter preceded by the reserved word var and followed by a specific type is called a *variable parameter*.

3. A parameter preceded by the reserved word var and *not* followed by a specific type is called an *untyped variable parameter*.

Value Parameters

Value parameters are completely local to the subroutine. Whenever the variable is used within the subroutine, the local *copy* of the variable is read or modified; the original variable (the actual parameter) is never touched.

Variable Parameters

A variable parameter is passed by *reference*: the procedure or function receives the address of the parameter. The address is used to access the actual variable, so that changes to the parameter result in changes to the variable itself.

Untyped Variable Parameters

Turbo Pascal allows you to bypass type-checking through the use of *untyped variable parameters*. One useful result of untyped variables is that you can use the same subroutine to process similar structures.

Forward Declarations

To reference a subroutine before it is defined, you perform a *forward* declaration *prior* to the first use of the subroutine.

The forward declaration is written exactly as the ordinary subroutine header, except that it's followed by the reserved word `forward`. Later, when the actual subroutine is defined, you don't need to repeat any of the parameters:

```
procedure LeftHand( a, b : word ); forward;

procedure RightHand( x, y, z : real );
begin
   LeftHand( 1, 2 );
end;

procedure LeftHand;
begin
   RightHand( 2.5, 4.8, 9.76 );
end;
```

Units and Overlays

A *program* is the main module of Turbo Pascal source code. A *unit* is simply a collection of subroutines that the program can invoke, but the unit is physically compiled, stored, loaded into memory, and accessed independently of the program itself.

Standard Units

In Turbo Pascal, the standard procedures and functions are stored in eight standard units, as follows:

System	Turbo Pascal's run-time library
Crt	Display and keyboard support
Dos	General DOS functions
Graph	Graphics support
Graph3	Implements Turbo Pascal 3.0 Turtlegraphics
Overlay	Implements the overlay manager
Printer	Allows you to easily access your printer
Turbo3	Compatibility with Turbo Pascal 3.0

The Graph unit resides in the GRAPH.TPU file. The Turbo3 and Graph3 units reside in the TURBO3.TPU and GRAPH3.TPU files respectively. All other standard units reside in the TURBO.TPL library file.

Except for the System unit, Turbo Pascal accesses each unit *only* when specifically directed. For example, if your program uses routines in the Crt and Dos units, then you *must* include a uses clause immediately after the program header, as follows:

```
uses Crt, Dos;
```

The Structure of a Unit

Each unit has four components—the header, interface, implementation, and initialization sections—arranged in the following manner:

```
unit identifier;
interface
uses list-of-units;   { Optional }
   { Public declarations of constants, types, and      }
   { variables intended to be accessible to the        }
   { user of the unit, plus the headings of            }
   { all public subroutines.                           }
implementation
uses list-of-units;   { Optional }
   { Private declarations of constants, types, and     }
   { variables intended to be inaccessible to the      }
   { user of the unit, including all private           }
   { procedures and functions in their entirety,       }
   { and the bodies of all subroutines declared in     }
   { the interface section.                            }
begin
   { Optional initialization statements                }
end.
```

Header

Every unit begins with a *unit header* similar in format to
a program header. As an example, the first line of a unit
named `Trig` would appear as follows:

```
unit Trig;
```

The presence of the reserved word `unit` tells the
compiler that the file *is* a unit and that when the unit is
compiled, its output file is to have .TPU for its extension.

Interface

The *interface* section declares every data object that you
want the unit to share with any program or calling unit.
Labels can't be declared because the target label of a
`goto` statement must be in the same block as the `goto`
statement. Only the *headers* of the procedures and
functions need to be declared. The bodies of the subroutines are defined in the `implementation` section.

If the unit needs to use another unit, *and* you wish the
other unit to also be available to the calling program,

then that other unit is declared in a `uses` clause at the
beginning of the `interface` section.

Implementation

The *implementation* section contains all of the procedures and functions that make the unit useful, including
the bodies of the subroutines whose headings were
previously declared in the `interface` section.

Since any constant, type, or variable declared in the
`interface` is global, it's automatically available to
the code in the `implementation` section. Additional
private declarations can be made in the `implementa-
tion` section, but they will be local to the unit.

If the unit needs to use another unit, *and* you don't wish
the other unit to be available to the calling program, then
that other unit is declared in a `uses` clause at the
beginning of the `implementation` section.

Initialization

Turbo Pascal provides a means for a unit to execute an
opening set of instructions—called *initialization code*—
before the first statement in the main program is
executed. Simply place all initialization codes at the end
of the `implementation` section, and preface the
statements with the reserved word `begin`.

Initialization code is optional. It is the presence of the
word `begin` that tells the compiler that initialization is
to be performed. If the main program `uses` several
units, each unit is initialized in the order in which it's
declared in the `uses` clause.

Creating Overlays

In Turbo Pascal, the smallest collection of overlaid
subroutines is the unit. Each unit is swapped into
memory prior to a call of a routine within the unit.

To convert a unit to an overlay, follow these steps:

1. Compile every overlay unit with the {$O+} directive enabled.

2. Compile every overlay unit and the main program itself with the {$F+} directive enabled.

3. The main program must have a `uses` statement that declares every unit to be overlayed as well as the Overlay standard unit itself. The Overlay standard unit must be named *before* any overlay units, as follows:

   ```
   uses Overlay, OvrSub1A, OvrSub2A;
   ```

4. Immediately following the `uses` clause, the main program must specify every unit to be overlayed with the {$O filename} directive, as follows:

   ```
   {$O OvrSub1A };
   {$O OvrSub2A };
   ```

5. The main program must execute the `OvrInit` overlay initiation procedure before any routine in any of the overlay units is invoked.

The Overlay unit defines the procedures `OvrInit`, `OvrInitEMS`, `OvrSetBuf`, and `OvrClearBuf`, and the function `OvrGetBuf`. You can test the result of any of these subroutines by examining the predefined integer variable `OvrResult`. The possible return values are provided in the following table together with several predefined constants, which can be used to make the test of `OvrResult` easier to understand.

Predefined Constant	Value	Typical Error Messages
ovrOk	0	NO ERROR
ovrError	-1	No overlays/buffer too small/heap not empty
ovrNotFound	-2	.OVR file wasn't found
ovrNoMemory	-3	Not enough heap space
ovrIOError	-4	I/O error reading overlay file
ovrNoEMSDriver	-5	EMS driver not installed
ovrNoEMSMemory	-6	Not enough EMS memory

Turbo Pascal 5.0 Standard Procedures and Functions

Abs

System

Syntax

```
Function Abs( X : AnyNumType ) :
    AnyNumType;
```

Purpose

Returns the absolute value of a variable. The result returned by the function has the same type as the argument, which may be any integer or real value.

Addr

System

Syntax

```
Function Addr( X : AnyDataObject ) :
    Pointer;
```

Purpose

Returns the address of the specified object. The argument may be a variable, procedure, or function identifier. The result is a pointer to the object. Note that the @ operator produces the same result as the `Addr` function.

Append

System

Syntax

```
Procedure Append( var FileIdentifier :
    Text );
```

Purpose

Opens an existing text file for appending. A run-time error is generated if the file can't be found. If the file doesn't already exist, you must first use Rewrite to create it.

Arc

Graph

Syntax

```
Procedure Arc( X, Y : Integer; StAng,
    EndAng, Radius : Word );
```

Purpose

Draws a circular arc of a specified Radius from starting angle StAng to ending angle EndAng, using (X, Y) as the center point. See also Circle, Ellipse, GetArcCoords, PieSlice, and Sector.

ArcTan

System

Syntax

```
Function ArcTan( X : Real ) : Real;
```

Purpose

Returns the angle, in radians, that has a tangent equal to the value of the argument.

Assign

System

Syntax

```
Procedure Assign( var FileIdentifier;
    FileName : String );
```

Purpose

Assigns the name of an external file to a file variable. The `FileIdentifier` variable may be declared for any file type. `FileName` is a string containing the name of the external file.

AssignCrt

Crt

Syntax

```
Procedure AssignCrt(var FileIdentifier
    : Text);
```

Purpose

Associates a text file with the CRT. The procedure is similar to the `Assign` standard procedure, except that instead of associating a `FileIdentifier` variable with an external file, `AssignCrt` associates the text file directly with the CRT.

Bar

Graph

Syntax

```
Procedure Bar(X1,Y1,X2,Y2 : Integer );
```

Purpose

Draws a bar using the current fill style and color. The upper left corner of the bar is at (X1, Y1) and the lower right corner is at (X2, Y2).

Bar3D

Graph

Syntax

```
Procedure Bar3D( X1, Y1, X2, Y2 :
    Integer; Depth : Word; Top :
    Boolean );
```

Purpose

Draws a 3-D bar using the current fill style and color. The upper left corner is at (X1, Y1), and the lower right corner is at (X2, Y2). Depth is the number of pixels used to define the thickness. If Top is True, a three-dimensional top appears on the bar.

BlockRead

System

Syntax

```
Procedure BlockRead( var FileIdent :
    file; var Buffer; Count : Word
    [; var Result : Word ] );
```

Purpose

Reads one or more records from `FileIdent` into the `Buffer`. `Count` or less records are read. The optional parameter `Result` contains the actual number of records written to the buffer.

`BlockRead` can only handle `complete` blocks. Partial blocks will not be transferred. Consequently, when you open the file with the `Reset` or `Rewrite` procedure, use the `RecSize` parameter to select a record size that divides evenly into the file size. Set the `RecSize` parameter to 1 for general file access.

BlockWrite

System

Syntax

```
Procedure BlockWrite( var FileIdent :
    file; var Buffer; Count : Word
    [; var Result : Word ] );
```

Purpose

Writes one or more records from a `Buffer` into `FileIdent`. `Count` or less records are transferred from memory. The optional parameter `Result` contains the number of records written to the buffer. `Block-Write` can handle only `complete` blocks. Partial blocks will not be transferred.

ChDir

System

Syntax

```
Procedure ChDir( NewPath : String );
```

Purpose

Changes the current directory to `NewPath`.

Chr

System

Syntax

```
Function Chr( X : Byte ) : Char;
```

Purpose

Returns the ASCII character for the specified ordinal number.

Circle

Graph

Syntax

```
Procedure Circle( X, Y : Integer;
   Radius : Word );
```

Purpose

Draws a circle of a specified `Radius` using (X, Y) as the center point.

ClearDevice

Graph

Syntax

```
Procedure ClearDevice;
```

Purpose

Clears the entire graphics screen using the current
background color, and moves the current pointer (CP)
to (0, 0).

ClearViewPort

Graph

Syntax

```
Procedure ClearViewPort;
```

Purpose

Clears the current viewport. The fill color is set to the
current background color. Bar is called using the
dimensions of the viewport as its parameters, and the
current pointer (CP) is moved to (0, 0).

Close

System

Syntax

```
Procedure Close( var FileIdentifier :
   AnyFileType );
```

Purpose

Closes an open file of any type. Closed files must be reopened with Reset, Rewrite, or Append before any
further input or output operations can take place, but it
isn't necessary to issue another Assign command.

CloseGraph

Graph

Syntax

```
Procedure CloseGraph;
```

Purpose

Shuts down the graphics system, restoring the screen to the mode it was in before graphics was initialized and deallocating any heap memory used by the graphics scan buffer, drivers, and fonts.

ClrEol

Crt

Syntax

```
Procedure ClrEol;
```

Purpose

Clears all characters from the cursor position to the end of the line. The position of the cursor isn't changed.

ClrScr

Crt

Syntax

```
Procedure ClrScr;
```

Purpose

Clears the current screen (or the current window, if one is active) using the current setting of TextBackground. The cursor is moved to (1,1).

Concat

System

Syntax

```
Function Concat( s1 [, s2, ..., sn ] :
    String ) : String;
```

Purpose

Concatenates a sequence of strings. The final string gets truncated if it exceeds 255 characters. Using the + operator produces the same result.

Copy

System

Syntax

```
Function Copy( Original : String;
    Index, Count : Integer ) : String;
```

Purpose

Returns a substring of the `Original` string, beginning at `Index`, containing `Count` characters.

Cos

System

Syntax

```
Function Cos( X : Real ) : Real;
```

Purpose

Returns the cosine of the argument. The input angle is measured in radians.

CSeg

System

Syntax

```
Function CSeg : Word;
```

Purpose

Returns the current value of the CS register.

Dec

System

Syntax

```
Procedure Dec( var X : OrdType [; n :
    LongInt ] );
```

Purpose

Decrements the value of any ordinal variable. If the optional parameter n isn't specified, then X is decremented by 1; otherwise, X is decremented by the value of n.

Delay

Crt

Syntax

```
Procedure Delay( MS : Word );
```

Purpose

Delays program execution for approximately MS milliseconds.

Delete

System

Syntax

```
Procedure Delete( var Original :
    String; Index, Count : Integer );
```

Purpose

Deletes `Count` characters from the `Original` string, beginning at `Index`.

DelLine

Crt

Syntax

```
Procedure DelLine;
```

Purpose

Deletes the line containing the cursor. All lines below the cursor are moved up one row, and a blank line appears at the bottom of the screen. The location of the cursor is unchanged.

DetectGraph

Graph

Syntax

```
Procedure DetectGraph( var
    GraphDriver, GraphMode :
    Integer );
```

Purpose

Checks the hardware installed in the PC and determines which graphics driver and mode to use. `GraphDriver` and `GraphMode` contain values that can then be passed to the `InitGraph` procedure. See `InitGraph` for a summary of valid drivers and modes.

DiskFree

Dos

Syntax

```
Function DiskFree( Drive : Byte ) :
    LongInt;
```

Purpose

Returns the number of free bytes on a specified disk drive. A Drive of 0 indicates the current drive, 1 indicates drive A:, 2 indicates drive B:, and so on. If Drive contains an invalid number, DiskFree returns -1.

DiskSize

Dos

Syntax

```
Function DiskSize( Drive : Byte ) :
    LongInt;
```

Purpose

Returns the total size in bytes on a specified disk drive. A `Drive` of 0 indicates the current drive, 1 indicates drive A:, 2 indicates drive B:, and so on. If `Drive` contains an invalid number, `DiskSize` returns -1.

Dispose

System

Syntax

```
Procedure Dispose( var P : Pointer );
```

Purpose

Disposes a dynamic variable allocated by the New procedure. The memory referenced by P is returned to the heap.

DosExitCode

Dos

Syntax

```
Function DosExitCode : Word;
```

Purpose

Returns the exit code of a subprocess. The low byte contains the code; the high byte indicates the reason the subprocess terminated: 0 for normal, 1 for Ctrl-C, 2 for a device error, and 3 if terminated by the Keep procedure. After DosExitCode is called, the code is set to zero.

DosVersion

Dos

Syntax

```
Function DosVersion : Word;
```

Purpose

Returns the DOS version number. The low and high bytes respectively contain the major and minor version.

DrawPoly

Graph

Syntax

```
Procedure DrawPoly( NumPoints : Word;
    var PolyPoints );
```

Purpose

Draws the outline of a polygon containing Num-
Points vertices, using the current line style and color.
PolyPoints is an array of PointType.

DSeg

System

Syntax

```
Function DSeg : Word;
```

Purpose

Returns the current value of the DS register, which
contains the segment address of the data segment.

Ellipse

Graph

Syntax

```
Procedure Ellipse( X, Y : Integer;
    StAngle, EndAngle, XRadius,
    YRadius : Word );
```

Purpose

Draws an elliptical arc from StAngle to EndAngle,
using (X, Y) as the center point. XRadius and

YRadius are the horizontal and vertical axes. Angles
are in degrees, running counterclockwise, with 0 degrees
at 3 o'clock.

EnvCount

Dos

Syntax

```
Function EnvCount : Integer;
```

Purpose

Returns the number of strings in the DOS environment.
Each string is in the form 'EnvStr = EnvValue'.

EnvStr

Dos

Syntax

```
Function EnvStr( Index : Integer ) :
    String;
```

Purpose

Returns a specified environment string. The first string
has an Index of 1.

Eof

System

Syntax

```
Function Eof[ ( var FileIdentifier :
    AnyFileType ) ] : Boolean;
```

Purpose

Returns the end-of-file status. Eof is True if the current file position is beyond the last character in the file, or if the file is empty; otherwise, Eof is False.

Eoln

System

Syntax

```
Function Eoln[ ( var FileIdentifier :
    Text ) ] : Boolean;
```

Purpose

Returns the end-of-line status of a file. Eoln is True if the current file position is at an end-of-line marker or if Eof is True; otherwise, Eoln is False. If no Text file FileIdentifier is provided, the standard Input file is assumed.

Erase

System

Syntax

```
Procedure Erase( var FileIdentifier :
    AnyFileType );
```

Purpose

Erases an unopened external file.

Exec

Dos

Syntax

```
Procedure Exec( Path : PathStr;
    ComLine : ComStr );
```

Purpose

Executes the program specified in the `Path` string with the command line contained in `ComLine`. The `PathStr` and `ComStr` types are defined as follows:

```
PathStr = String[79];
ComStr  = String[127];
```

Exit

System

Syntax

```
Procedure Exit;
```

Purpose

Exits immediately from the current block or subroutine. When used within the main body of a program, `Exit` causes the program to terminate.

Exp

System

Syntax

```
Function Exp( X : Real ) : Real;
```

Purpose

Returns the natural number e raised to the power of X.

FExpand

Dos

Syntax

```
Function FExpand( Path : PathStr ) :
    PathStr;
```

Purpose

Expands a file name into a fully qualified file name, consisting of the drive, path, and file name. FExpand isn't needed if your program only uses the current directory.

FilePos

System

Syntax

```
Function FilePos( var FileIdentifier )
    : LongInt;
```

Purpose

Returns the current record number of an opened file. FilePos cannot be used on a text file.

FileSize

System

Syntax

```
Function FileSize( var FileIdentifier
    : AnyFileType ) : LongInt;
```

Purpose

Returns the number of components in an opened file. If the file is empty, `FileSize` returns 0. `FileSize` cannot be used on a text file.

FillChar

System

Syntax

```
Procedure FillChar( var X : AnyType;
   Count : Word; Ch : AnyOrdType );
```

Purpose

Fills a variable X (declared to be of any type) with `Count` characters of `Ch`, which may be any ordinal type. No range checking is performed.

FillEllipse

Graph

Syntax

```
Procedure FillEllipse( X, Y : Integer;
   XRadius, YRadius : Word );
```

Purpose

Draws a filled ellipse, centered at (X, Y), having horizontal and vertical axes of `XRadius` and `YRadius` respectively.

FillPoly

Graph

Syntax

```
Procedure FillPoly( NumPoints : Word;
    var PolyPoints );
```

Purpose

Draws and fills a polygon containing NumPoints vertices, using the current fill style and color.

FindFirst

Dos

Syntax

```
Procedure FindFirst( Path : PathStr;
    Attr : Word; var F : SearchRec );
```

Purpose

Searches the Path directory mask for the first file having the attributes specified by Attr. The SearchRec record F is used as input for the Find-Next procedure. See GetFAttr for a discussion of the file attribute parameter Attr. See GetFTime for a discussion of the Time parameter.

FindNext

Dos

Syntax

```
Procedure FindNext( var F:SearchRec );
```

Purpose

> Returns the next entry that matches the name and attributes specified in the SearchRec record F, obtained from a previous call to FindFirst.

FloodFill

Graph

Syntax

```
Procedure FloodFill( X, Y : Integer;
   Border : Word );
```

Purpose

> Fills a region containing the point (X, Y) and bounded by the Border color.

Flush

System

Syntax

```
Procedure Flush( var FileIdentifier :
   Text );
```

Purpose

> Flushes the buffer of a text file open for output, forcing any data in the buffer to be immediately saved to disk.

Frac

System

Syntax

```
Function Frac( X : Real ) : Real;
```

Purpose

Returns the fractional part of the argument.

FreeMem

System

Syntax

```
Procedure FreeMem( var P : Pointer;
    Size : Word );
```

Purpose

Disposes (that is, deallocates) a dynamic variable P of a given Size, which was previously created by a call to the GetMem procedure.

FSearch

Dos

Syntax

```
Function FSearch( Path : PathStr;
    DirList : String ) : PathStr;
```

Purpose

Searches for a file given by Path in a list of directories given by DirList.

FSplit

Dos

Syntax

```
Procedure FSplit( Path : PathStr; var
    Dir : DirStr; var Name : NameStr;
    var Ext  : ExtStr );
```

Purpose

Splits the file name specified by `Path` into its three components; the drive and directory are placed in `Dir`, the file name in `Name`, and the extension in `Ext`.

GetArcCoords

Graph

Syntax

```
Procedure GetArcCoords( var ArcCoords
    : ArcCoordsType );
```

Purpose

Allows the user to inquire about the coordinates of the last `Arc` or `Ellipse` command. `GetArcCoords` returns a record of the type `ArcCoordsType`.

GetAspectRatio

Graph

Syntax

```
Procedure GetAspectRatio( var Xasp,
    Yasp : Word );
```

Purpose

Get the effective resolution of the graphics screen. The aspect ratio can be computed by dividing the `Xasp` parameter by the `Yasp` parameter.

GetBkColor

Graph

Syntax

```
Function GetBkColor : Word;
```

Purpose

Returns the index into the palette of the current background color.

GetCBreak

Dos

Syntax

```
Procedure GetCBreak( var Break :
    Boolean );
```

Purpose

Returns the state of Ctrl-Break checking in DOS. When off (`Break` = False), DOS tests for Ctrl-Break only during I/O operations; when on (`Break` = True), DOS tests for Ctrl-Break before every system call.

GetColor

Syntax

```
Function GetColor : Word;
```

Purpose

Returns the color value passed to the previous successful call to SetColor.

GetDate

Syntax

```
Procedure GetDate( var Year, Month,
    Day, DayOfWeek : Word );
```

Purpose

Returns the current date set in the operating system.

GetDefaultPalette

Syntax

```
Procedure GetDefaultPalette( var
    Palette : PaletteType );
```

Purpose

Returns the Palette definition record of the type
PaletteType.

GetDir

System

Syntax

```
Procedure GetDir( DriveNumber : Byte;
    var DirString : String );
```

Purpose

Returns the current directory DirString of a
specified DriveNumber. A DriveNumber of
0 indicates the current drive, 1 indicates drive A:,
2 indicates drive B:, and so on.

GetDriverName

Graph

Syntax

```
Function GetDriverName : String;
```

Purpose

Returns a string containing the name of the current
driver.

GetEnv

Dos

Syntax

```
Function GetEnv( EnvVar : String ) :
    String;
```

Purpose

Returns the value of a specified environment variable.

GetFAttr

Dos

Syntax

```
Procedure GetFAttr( var F :
    AnyFileType; var Attr : Word );
```

Purpose

Returns the attributes of an unopened file. The file, F, can be tested for an individual attribute by logically ANDing the Attr parameter with one of the following predefined constants:

```
ReadOnly  = $01;
Hidden    = $02;
SysFile   = $04;
VolumeID  = $08;
Directory = $10;
Archive   = $20;
AnyFile   = $3F;
```

The predefined constant AnyFile is the sum of all other constants and consequently can be used for performing multiple comparisons.

GetFillPattern

Graph

Syntax

```
Procedure GetFillPattern( var
    FillPattern : FillPatternType );
```

Purpose

Returns an array containing the fill pattern set by the most recent call to SetFillPattern.

GetFillSettings

Graph

Syntax
```
Procedure GetFillSettings( var
    FillInfo : FillSettingsType );
```

Purpose

Returns the last fill pattern and color set by a previous call to SetFillStyle.

GetFTime

Dos

Syntax
```
Procedure GetFTime( var F :
    AnyFileType; var Time : LongInt );
```

Purpose

Returns the date and time a file F was last written. Time may be unpacked and read with the UnpackTime procedure. See also GetFAttr and SetFTime.

The long integer Time contains the packed format of the time and date of the last write operation on the file. The high-order word is the date stamp, which is stored in the format:

Bits	Contents	Value
0 - 4	Day of month	1 to 31
5 - 8	Month	1 to 12
9 - 15	Year	(Year - 1980)

GetGraphMode

Graph

Syntax
```
Function GetGraphMode : Integer;
```

Purpose

Returns the current graphics mode.

GetImage

Graph

Syntax
```
Procedure GetImage( X1, Y1, X2, Y2 :
    Integer; var BitMap );
```

Purpose

Saves into BitMap a bit image of the screen bounded by X1, Y1 (upper left corner) and X2, Y2 (lower right corner).

GetIntVec

Dos

Syntax
```
Procedure GetIntVec( IntNo : Byte; var
    Vector : Pointer );
```

Purpose

Returns the address stored in a specified interrupt vector. See also SetIntVec.

GetLineSettings

Graph

Syntax

```
Procedure GetLineSettings( var
    LineInfo : LineSettingsType );
```

Purpose

Returns a `LineInfo` record containing the current line style, pattern, and thickness as set by `SetLineStyle`.

GetMaxColor

Graph

Syntax

```
Function GetMaxColor : Word;
```

Purpose

Returns the highest color that can be passed to the `SetColor` procedure. See also `GetPaletteSize`.

GetMaxMode

Graph

Syntax

```
Function GetMaxMode : Integer;
```

Purpose

Returns the maximum mode number for the currently loaded driver. See also `GetModeRange`.

GetMaxX

Graph

Syntax

```
Function GetMaxX : Integer;
```

Purpose

Returns the rightmost column (X resolution) of the current graphics driver and mode.

GetMaxY

Graph

Syntax

```
Function GetMaxY : Integer;
```

Purpose

Returns the bottommost row (Y resolution) of the current graphics driver and mode.

GetMem

System

Syntax

```
Procedure GetMem( var P : Pointer;
    Size : Word );
```

Purpose

Creates a new dynamic variable of the specified Size and puts its address in the pointer variable P.

GetModeName

Graph

Syntax

```
Function GetModeName( GraphMode :
    Integer ) : String;
```

Purpose

Returns a string containing the name of the specified graphics mode.

GetModeRange

Graph

Syntax

```
Procedure GetModeRange( GraphDriver :
    Integer; var LoMode, HiMode :
    Integer );
```

Purpose

Returns the lowest and highest valid graphics modes for a given driver.

GetPalette

Graph

Syntax

```
Procedure GetPalette( var Palette :
    PaletteType );
```

Purpose

Returns the current palette and its size in the Palette record.

GetPaletteSize

Graph

Syntax

```
Function GetPaletteSize : Integer;
```

Purpose

Returns the size of the palette color lookup table.

GetPixel

Graph

Syntax

```
Function GetPixel( X, Y : Integer ) :
    Word;
```

Purpose

Gets the color of the pixel at (X, Y).

GetTextSettings

Graph

Syntax

```
Procedure GetTextSettings( var
    TextInfo : TextSettingsType );
```

Purpose

Returns the current text font, direction, size, and justification as set by SetTextStyle and SetTextJustify.

GetTime

Dos

Syntax

```
Procedure GetTime( var Hour, Minute,
    Second, Sec100 : Word );
```

Purpose

Returns the current time set in the operating system.

GetVerify

Dos

Syntax

```
Procedure GetVerify( var Verify :
    Boolean );
```

Purpose

Returns the state of the verify flag in DOS. When off
(Verify = False), disk writes aren't verified. When on
(Verify = True), all disk writes are verified.

GetViewSettings

Graph

Syntax

```
Procedure GetViewSettings( var
    ViewPort : ViewPortType );
```

Purpose

Returns the current viewport and clipping settings as
set by SetViewPort.

GetX

Graph

Syntax

```
Function GetX : Integer;
```

Purpose

Returns the X coordinate of the current position (CP).

GetY

Graph

Syntax

```
Function GetY : Integer;
```

Purpose

Returns the Y coordinate of the current position (CP).

GotoXY

Crt

Syntax

```
Procedure GotoXY( X, Y : Byte );
```

Purpose

Positions the cursor at (X, Y).

GraphDefaults

Graph

Syntax

```
Procedure GraphDefaults;
```

Purpose

Resets the graphics settings for the viewport; palette; draw and background colors; line style and pattern; fill style, color, and pattern; active font; text style; text justification; and user character size.

GraphErrorMsg

Graph

Syntax

```
Function GraphErrorMsg( ErrorCode :
    Integer ) : String;
```

Purpose

Returns the error message corresponding to the specified ErrorCode. See GraphResult for a list of possible messages.

GraphResult

Graph

Syntax

```
Function GraphResult : Integer;
```

Purpose

Returns an error code for the last graphics operation.
The returned value will be equal to one of the following predefined constants:

Constant Name	Error Code	Description
grOk	0	No error
grNoInitGraph	-1	(BGI) graphics not installed
grNotDetected	-2	Graphics hardware not detected
grFileNotFound	-3	Device driver file not found ( )
grInvalidDriver	-4	Invalid device driver file ( )
grNoLoadMem	-5	Not enough memory to load driver
grNoScanMem	-6	Out of memory in scan fill
grNoFloodMem	-7	Out of memory in flood fill
grFontNotFound	-8	Font file not found ( )
grNoFontMem	-9	Not enough memory to load font
grInvalidMode	-10	Invalid graphics mode for selected driver
grError	-11	Graphics error
grIOerror	-12	Graphics I/O error
grInvalidFont	-13	Invalid font file ( )
grInvalidFontNum	-14	Invalid font number

The error code is reset to 0 after `GraphResult` is
completed.

Halt

System

Syntax

```
Procedure Halt[( ExitCode : Word )];
```

Purpose

Stops program execution and returns to the operating
system. The optional parameter `ExitCode` specifies

the exit code of the program. When ExitCode is
omitted, Halt(0) is assumed.

Hi

System

Syntax

```
Function Hi( X : IntWord ) : Byte;
```

Purpose

Returns the high-order byte of the argument, which
may be either an Integer or a Word.

HighVideo

Crt

Syntax

```
Procedure HighVideo;
```

Purpose

Causes all subsequent screen output to appear in high-
intensity characters.

ImageSize

Graph

Syntax

```
Function ImageSize( X1, Y1, X2, Y2 :
    Integer ) : Word;
```

Purpose

Returns the number of bytes required to store the portion of the screen with upper left coordinates of (X1, Y1) and lower right coordinates of (X2, Y2).

Inc

Syntax

```
Procedure Inc( var X : OrdType [; n :
    LongInt ] );
```

Purpose

Increments the value of any ordinal variable. If the parameter n isn't specified, then X is incremented by 1; otherwise, X is incremented by the value of n.

InitGraph

Syntax

```
Procedure InitGraph( var GraphDriver :
    Integer; var GraphMode : Integer;
    PathToDriver : String );
```

Purpose

Initializes the graphics system. If InitGraph is called when GraphDriver is equal to Detect (a predefined constant of 0), then InitGraph automatically selects an appropriate graphics driver and an optimal mode based on its analysis of the configuration of the PC. Otherwise, if GraphDriver is not equal to 0, InitGraph assumes that GraphDriver specifies a particular graphics driver and that `GraphMode` specifies a particular mode.

Graphics drivers, which physically reside in .BGI files, are selected by setting the `GraphDriver` parameter equal to one of the following predefined constants:

Predefined Constant	Value	Graphics Adapter
Detect	0	—
CGA	1	Color Graphics Adapter
MCGA	2	Multicolor Graphics Array
EGA	3	Enhanced Graphics Adapter
EGA64	4	Enhanced Graphics Adapter
EGAMono	5	Enhanced Graphics Adapter
IBM8514	6	IBM 8514 Graphics
HercMono	7	Hercules Monochrome Graphics
ATT400	8	AT&T 400 Line Graphics
VGA	9	Video Graphics Adapter
PC3270	10	IBM PC 3270 Graphics

A valid mode for a driver is selected by setting `Graph-Mode` to one of the following predefined constants:

Graphics Adapter	Constant Name	Value	Resolution (ColxRow)	Palette
CGA	CGAC0	0	320×200	C0
	CGAC1	1	320×200	C1
	CGAC2	2	320×200	C2
	CGAC3	3	320×200	C3
	CGAHi	4	640×200	2 colors
MCGA	MCGAC0	0	320×200	C0
	MCGAC1	1	320×200	C1
	MCGAC2	2	320×200	C2
	MCGAC3	3	320×200	C3
	MCGAMed	4	640×200	2 colors
	MCGAHi	5	640×480	2 colors
EGA	EGALo	0	640×200	16 colors
	EGAHi	1	640×350	16 colors
	EGA64Lo	0	640×200	16 colors
	EGA64Hi	1	640×350	4 colors
	EGAMonoHi	3	640×350	2 colors
	EGAMonoHi	3	640×350	2 colors

Graphics Adapter	Constant Name	Value	Resolution (ColxRow)	Palette
Hercules	HercMonoHi	0	720×348	2 colors
AT&T	ATT400C0	0	320×200	C0
	ATT400C1	1	320×200	C1
	ATT400C2	2	320×200	C2
	ATT400C3	3	320×200	C3
	ATT400Med	4	640×200	2 colors
	ATT400Hi	5	640×400	2 colors
VGA	VGALo	0	640×200	16 colors
	VGAMed	1	640×350	16 colors
	VGAHi	2	640×480	16 colors
3270 PC	PC3270Hi	0	720×350	2 colors
IBM 8514	IBM8514LO	0	640×480	256 colors
	IBM8514HI	1	1024×768	256 colors

The `PathToDriver` string contains the name of the directory containing the graphics driver files. If `Path-ToDriver` is empty, the driver files must be in the current directory.

If `InitGraph` is successful, it loads the .BGI driver file into heap memory, enters graphics mode, initializes all graphics settings to their defaults, and clears the screen. CGA, MCGA, and AT&T adapters can display a maximum of only four colors, selected from one of the following palettes:

Palette	Color 0	Color 1	Color 2	Color 3
C0	Background	LtGreen	LtRed	Yellow
C1	Background	LtCyan	LtMagenta	White
C2	Background	Green	Red	Brown
C3	Background	Cyan	Magenta	LtGray

If your PC uses a CGA, MCGA, or AT&T adapter, `InitGraph` will default to the high-resolution, monochrome mode. If you want to display the full four-color palette on your screen, then you will have to `select` a specific mode.

Insert

System

Syntax
```
Procedure Insert( Source:String; var
    Target:String; Index:Integer );
```

Purpose
Inserts a Source string into a Target string, beginning at the Index position. If the resulting string would
exceed 255 characters, it will be truncated after the
255th character.

InsLine

Crt

Syntax
```
Procedure InsLine;
```

Purpose
Inserts an empty line at the cursor position.

InstallUserDriver

Graph

Syntax
```
Function InstallUserDriver(
    DriverFileName : String;
    AutoDetectPtr : Pointer ) :
    Integer;
```

Purpose

Adds the device driver called `DriverFileName` to the .BGI device driver table. `AutoDetectPtr` is a pointer to an accompanying autodetect function (if any).

InstallUserFont

Graph

Syntax

```
Function InstallUserFont( FontFileName
    : String ) : Integer;
```

Purpose

Installs into the .BGI system a new font called `FontFileName`.

Int

System

Syntax

```
Function Int( X : Real ) : Real;
```

Purpose

Returns the integer part of a real-type argument.

Intr

Dos

Syntax

```
Procedure Intr( IntNo : Byte; var Regs
   : Registers );
```

Purpose

Executes BIOS interrupt number IntNo. Any parameters are passed with a record of the type Registers.

IOResult

System

Syntax

```
Function IOResult : Word;
```

Purpose

If I/O checking is disabled with {$I-}, IOResult returns and resets the value of the internal error flag for the last I/O operation. A value of 0 indicates success; nonzero indicates that an error occurred. The possible values returned by IOResult are:

DOS Errors

2	File not found.
3	Path not found.
4	Too many open files.
5	File access denied.
6	Invalid file handle.
12	Invalid file access code.
15	Invalid drive number.
16	Cannot remove current directory.
17	Cannot rename across drives.

I/O Errors

100	Disk read error.
101	Disk write error.
102	File not assigned.
103	File not open.
104	File not open for input.
105	File not open for output.
106	Invalid numeric format.

Critical Errors

150	Disk is write-protected.
151	Unknown unit.
152	Drive not ready.
153	Unknown command.
154	CRC error in data.
155	Bad drive request structure length.
156	Disk seek error.
157	Unknown media type.
158	Sector not found.
159	Printer out of paper.
160	Device write fault.
161	Device read fault.
162	Hardware failure.

Keep

Dos

Syntax

```
Procedure Keep( ExitCode : Word );
```

Purpose

Terminates the current program and makes it—in its entirety—stay resident in memory. ExitCode corresponds to the exit code parameter used in the Halt procedure. See also DosExitCode.

KeyPressed

Crt

Syntax
```
Function KeyPressed : Boolean;
```

Purpose
Returns True if a key has been pressed, or False otherwise. Shift, Ctrl, and Alt, etc. are ignored.

Length

System

Syntax
```
Function Length( Str : String ) :
    Integer;
```

Purpose
Returns the active length of the Str string.

Line

Graph

Syntax
```
Procedure Line( X1, Y1, X2, Y2 :
    Integer );
```

Purpose
Draws a line from (X1, Y1) to (X2, Y2) using the line style and thickness set by SetLineStyle and the color set by SetColor.

LineRel

Graph

Syntax

```
Procedure LineRel( Dx, Dy : Integer );
```

Purpose

Draws a line to a point located a relative distance from the current pointer (CP) using the line style and thickness set by SetLineStyle and the color set by SetColor.

LineTo

Graph

Syntax

```
Procedure LineTo( X, Y : Integer );
```

Purpose

Draws a line from the current pointer (CP) to (X, Y) using the line style and thickness set by SetLine-Style and the color set by SetColor.

Ln

System

Syntax

```
Function Ln( X : Real ) : Real;
```

Purpose

Returns the natural logarithm of the argument, which must be positive.

Lo

System

Syntax

```
Function Lo( X : IntWord ) : Byte;
```

Purpose

Returns the low-order byte of the argument, which may be either an Integer or a Word.

LowVideo

Crt

Syntax

```
Procedure LowVideo;
```

Purpose

Causes all subsequent screen output to use low-intensity characters.

Mark

System

Syntax

```
Procedure Mark( var P : Pointer );
```

Purpose

Copies the current value of HeapPtr to the pointer variable P.

MaxAvail

System

Syntax
```
Function MaxAvail : LongInt;
```

Purpose
Returns the size, in bytes, of the largest contiguous free block in the heap.

MemAvail

System

Syntax
```
Function MemAvail : LongInt;
```

Purpose
Returns the sum, in bytes, of all free blocks in the heap.

MkDir

System

Syntax
```
Procedure MkDir( SubName : String );
```

Purpose
Creates a subdirectory specified by SubName.

Move

System

Syntax

```
Procedure Move( var Source,
    Destination; Count : Word );
```

Purpose

Copies `Count` contiguous bytes from `Source` to `Destination`.

MoveRel

Graph

Syntax

```
Procedure MoveRel( Dx, Dy : Integer );
```

Purpose

Moves the current pointer (CP) a relative distance from its starting location.

MoveTo

Graph

Syntax

```
Procedure MoveTo( X, Y : Integer );
```

Purpose

Moves the current pointer (CP) to (X, Y).

MsDos

Dos

Syntax

```
Procedure MsDos(var Regs: Registers);
```

Purpose

Executes a DOS function call with interrupt $21.

New

System

Syntax

```
Procedure New( var P : Pointer );
```

Purpose

Allocates enough space in the heap for a dynamic
variable of the type pointed to by P and sets P to the
address of the new variable.

NormVideo

Crt

Syntax

```
Procedure NormVideo;
```

Purpose

Selects the original text attribute read from the cursor
location when the program began.

NoSound

Crt

Syntax

```
Procedure NoSound;
```

Purpose

Turns off the internal speaker.

Odd

System

Syntax

```
Function Odd( X : LongInt ) : Boolean;
```

Purpose

Returns True if the argument is an odd number;
otherwise, False is returned.

Ofs

System

Syntax

```
Function Ofs( X : AnyType ) : Word;
```

Purpose

Returns the offset of the specified object. See also
Addr, Ptr, and Seg.

Ord

System

Syntax

```
Function Ord( X : OrdType ) : LongInt;
```

Purpose

Returns the ordinal number of any ordinal-type value.

OutText

Graph

Syntax

```
Procedure OutText(TextString: String);
```

Purpose

Outputs TextString to the location of the current
pointer (CP).

OutTextXY

Graph

Syntax

```
Procedure OutTextXY( X, Y : Integer;
    TextString : String );
```

Purpose

Outputs TextString to the location (X, Y).

OvrClearBuf

Overlay

Syntax

```
Procedure OvrClearBuf;
```

Purpose

Clears the overlay buffer, forcing all subsequent calls to overlaid routines to be reloaded from the overlay file (or from EMS memory).

OvrGetBuf

Overlay

Syntax

```
Function OvrGetBuf : LongInt;
```

Purpose

Returns the current size of the overlay buffer.

OvrInit

Overlay

Syntax

```
Procedure OvrInit(FileName : String);
```

Purpose

Initializes the overlay manager and opens the overlay file called FileName.

OvrInitEMS

Overlay

Syntax

```
Procedure OvrInitEMS;
```

Purpose

If an EMS driver and adequate EMS memory are detected, then OvrInitEMS loads the overlay file into EMS and closes the overlay file on disk.

OvrSetBuf

Overlay

Syntax

```
Procedure OvrSetBuf( Size : LongInt );
```

Purpose

Resets the size of the overlay buffer.

PackTime

Dos

Syntax

```
Procedure PackTime( var T : DateTime;
    var P : LongInt );
```

Purpose

Converts a DateTime record into a 4-byte, packed date-and-time longint used by SetFTime. No range-checking is performed on the fields. See GetFTime for a discussion of the format of the P parameter.

ParamCount

System

Syntax

```
Function ParamCount : Word;
```

Purpose

Returns the number of command-line parameters passed to the program.

ParamStr

System

Syntax

```
Function ParamStr(Index: Word) :
    String;
```

Purpose

Returns the command-line parameter specified by Index.

Pi

System

Syntax

```
Function Pi : Real;
```

Purpose

Returns the value of Pi (3.1415926535897932385).

PieSlice

Graph

Syntax

```
Procedure PieSlice( X, Y : Integer;
    StAngle, EndAngle, Radius : Word );
```

Purpose

Draws and fills a pie slice of a specified Radius, centered at (X, Y) and extending from StAngle to EndAngle.

Pos

System

Syntax

```
Function Pos( SubStr, Str : String ) :
    Byte;
```

Purpose

Searches for the substring SubStr in a string Str. Returns the index if SubStr is found, or 0 if not.

Pred

System

Syntax

```
Function Pred( X : OrdType ) :
    OrdType;
```

Purpose

Returns the predecessor of the argument, which can be any ordinal type.

Ptr

System

Syntax

```
Function Ptr( Seg, Ofs : Word ) :
    Pointer;
```

Purpose

Converts a segment base and an offset address to a pointer compatible with all pointer types.

PutImage

Graph

Syntax

```
Procedure PutImage( X, Y : Integer;
    var BitMap; DisplayOption:Word );
```

Purpose

Copies contents of BitMap to the screen at X, Y (upper left corner). Values for DisplayOption are

CopyPut	0	{ MOV }
XORPut	1	{ XOR }
OrPut	2	{ OR }
AndPut	3	{ AND }
NotPut	4	{ NOT }

PutPixel

Graph

Syntax

```
Procedure PutPixel( X, Y : Integer;
    PixelColor : Word );
```

Purpose

Sets the pixel at (X, Y) to the color of PixelColor.

Random

System

Syntax 1

```
Function Random : Real;
```

Syntax 2

```
Function Random( [ Range : Word ] ) :
    Word;
```

Purpose

Returns a random number. If Range isn't specified,
Random returns a real-type random number within the
range 0 <= x < 1. When Range is used, Random
returns a word-type random number within the range
0 <= x < Range.

Randomize

System

Syntax

```
Procedure Randomize;
```

Purpose

Initializes the predefined variable RandSeed with a
random value taken from the system clock.

Read

System

Syntax

```
Procedure Read( [var FileID :
    FileType;] v1 [,v2,...,vn] );
```

Purpose

Reads one or more values from a file into one or more variables. If `FileID` is omitted, the standard text file `Input` is assumed.

ReadKey

Crt

Syntax

```
Function ReadKey : Char;
```

Purpose

Reads a character from the keyboard without echoing it to the screen.

Readln

System

Syntax

```
Procedure Readln( [var FileID : Text;]
    v1 [,v2,...,vn] );
```

Purpose

Executes the `Read` procedure, then skips to the next line of the file. `FileID`, if specified, must be a text file; if omitted, the standard text file `Input` is assumed.

Rectangle

Graph

Syntax

```
Procedure Rectangle( X1, Y1, X2, Y2 :
    Integer );
```

Purpose

Draws a rectangle in the current line style and color, with upper left and lower right corners at (X1, Y1) and (X2, Y2), respectively.

RegisterBGIdriver

Graph

Syntax

```
Function RegisterBGIdriver( Driver :
    Pointer ) : Integer;
```

Purpose

Registers a user-loaded or linked-in BGI driver with the graphics system.

RegisterBGIfont

Graph

Syntax

```
Function RegisterBGIfont( Font :
    Pointer ) : Integer;
```

Purpose

Registers a user-loaded or linked-in BGI font with the graphics system.

Release

System

Syntax

```
Procedure Release( var P : Pointer );
```

Purpose

Sets the top of the heap to the location P.

Rename

System

Syntax

```
Procedure Rename( var F; NewName :
    String );
```

Purpose

Renames an unopened external file to NewName.

Reset

System

Syntax

```
Procedure Reset( var F [ : file;
    RecSize : Word ] );
```

Purpose

If F is declared as a text file, Reset opens it for input.
If F is declared as typed or untyped, Reset opens it
for input and output. RecSize can be used only if F is
declared as an untyped file; it specifies the record size
used for data transfers. If RecSize is not used, the
default is 128 bytes.

RestoreCrtMode

Graph

Syntax

```
Procedure RestoreCrtMode;
```

Purpose

Restores the screen to its original mode before
InitGraph initialized graphics.

Rewrite

System

Syntax

```
Procedure Rewrite( var F [ : file;
    RecSize : Word ] );
```

Purpose

Creates and opens file. If F is declared as a text file,
Rewrite opens it for output only. If F is declared as a
typed or untyped file, Rewrite opens it for both input
and output.

Rewrite first searches for the DOS file specified in
the Assign statement. If the file already exists,
Rewrite deletes it, then creates a new file with the
same name. If the file doesn't exist, Rewrite creates
it. This ensures that the file is always empty and that
output starts at the *beginning* of the file.

The optional RecSize parameter, which can be used
only if F is declared as a untyped file, specifies the
record size used for data transfers; if RecSize is
omitted, Rewrite uses a default record size of 128
bytes.

RmDir

System

Syntax

```
Procedure RmDir( EmptyDir : String );
```

Purpose

Removes an empty subdirectory specified by EmptyDir.

Round

System

Syntax

```
Function Round( X : Real ) : LongInt;
```

Purpose

Rounds a real-type value to an integer-type value.

RunError

System

Syntax

```
Procedure RunError[ ( ErrorCode :
Word ) ];
```

Purpose

Halts program execution and generates a run-time error. If the optional parameter ErrorCode is omitted, the run-time error number is assumed to be 0.

Sector

Graph

Syntax

```
Procedure Sector( X, Y : Integer;
    StAngle, EndAngle, XRadius,
    YRadius: Word );
```

Purpose

Draws and fills an elliptical sector from starting angle StAngle to ending angle EndAngle, using (X, Y) as the center point. XRadius and YRadius are the horizontal and vertical axes respectively. Angles are measured in degrees, running counterclockwise with 0 degrees at the 3 o'clock position. The outline of the sector is drawn in the current color. The interior of the sector is filled with the pattern and color specified by SetFillStyle or SetFillPattern.

Seek

System

Syntax

```
Procedure Seek( var F; CompNumber :
    LongInt );
```

Purpose

Moves the current position of an opened file F to the specified component CompNumber. The file variable F may reference a typed or untyped file but not a text file. For a typed file, the component is the same data object as the type of the file. For an untyped file, the component is a record whose size defaults to 128 bytes; the size may be changed by the optional RecSize parameter of the Reset or Rewrite procedure that opens it. The first component of the file is always number 0.

Executing the command `Seek( F, FileSize(F))` positions the file pointer one record *beyond* the end of the file. This causes all subsequent `Write` or `BlockWrite` procedures to append their data to the existing file.

SeekEof

System

Syntax

```
Function SeekEof[ ( var F : Text ) ] :
    Boolean;
```

Purpose

Returns the end-of-file status of a text file. `SeekEof` behaves like `Eof` except that it ignores all blanks, tabs, and end-of-line markers.

SeekEoln

System

Syntax

```
Function SeekEoln[ ( var F : Text ) ]
    : Boolean;
```

Purpose

Returns the end-of-line status of a text file. `SeekEoln` behaves like `Eoln`, except that blanks and tabs are ignored.

Seg

System

Syntax

```
Function Seg( X : AnyType ) : Word;
```

Purpose

Returns the segment of a specified object.

SetActivePage

Graph

Syntax

```
Procedure SetActivePage(Page: Word);
```

Purpose

Selects Page as the active page for receiving all subsequent graphics output.

Multiple pages (that is, page numbers other than 0) are only supported by EGA (256K), VGA, and Hercules graphics adapters, as follows. Each driver file has the extension BGI.

Graphics Driver	Mode Name	Value	Res	Clrs	Pg
EGA					
EGAVGA	EGALo	0	640×200	16	4
	EGAHi	1	640×350	16	2
	EGAMonoHi	3	640×350	2	2
Hercules					
HERC	HercMonoHi	0	720×348	2	2
VGA					
EGAVGA	VGALo	0	640×200	16	4
	VGAMed	1	640×350	16	2

The `SetActivePage` procedure will be ignored if it is executed when any other driver or mode is active. See also `SetVisualPage`.

SetAllPalette

Graph

Syntax

```
Procedure SetAllPalette(var Palette);
```

Purpose

Changes all palette colors as specified. `Palette` is an untyped parameter, but usually conforms to the `PaletteType` record. The `Size` byte specifies the length of the active part of the structure.

SetAspectRatio

Graph

Syntax

```
Procedure SetAspectRatio( Xasp, Yasp :
Word );
```

Purpose

Changes the default aspect ratio of the current graphics mode to `Xasp` / `Yasp`.

SetBkColor

Graph

Syntax

```
Procedure SetBkColor( ColorNum:Word );
```

Purpose

Sets the background color to ColorNum (from 0 to 15).

SetCBreak

Dos

Syntax

```
Procedure SetCBreak( Break:Boolean );
```

Purpose

Sets the state of Ctrl-Break checking in DOS. If SetCBreak is called when Break is False, DOS will check for Ctrl-Break during I/O operations only. If SetCBreak is called when Break is True, DOS will check for Ctrl-Break at every system call. See also GetCBreak.

SetColor

Graph

Syntax

```
Procedure SetColor( ColorNum : Word );
```

Purpose

Sets the current drawing color to ColorNum (from 0 to 15.

SetDate

Dos

Syntax

```
Procedure SetDate( Year, Month, Day :
    Word );
```

Purpose

Sets the current date in the operating system.

SetFAttr

Dos

Syntax

```
Procedure SetFAttr( var F :
    AnyFileType; Attr : Word );
```

Purpose

Sets the attributes of the unopened file F. See GetF-
Attr for a discussion of file attribute values for Attr.

SetFillPattern

Graph

Syntax

```
Procedure SetFillPattern( Pattern :
    FillPatternType; Color : Word );
```

Purpose

Selects a user-defined fill Pattern and Color. The
pattern is formed as an 8×8 grid of pixels corresponding
to the 64 bits contained in the FillPatternType
array.

SetFillStyle

Graph

Syntax

```
Procedure SetFillStyle( Pattern,
    ColorNum : Word );
```

Purpose

Sets the fill pattern and color. The `Pattern` parameter may be chosen from among the following predefined constants:

Constant Name	Value	Description
EmptyFill	0	Uses the background color
SolidFill	1	Uses a solid fill color
LineFill	2	— fill pattern
LtSlashFill	3	/// fill pattern
SlashFill	4	/// fill pattern (thick lines)
BkSlashFill	5	\\\ fill pattern (thick lines)
LtBkSlashFill	6	\\\ fill pattern
HatchFill	7	Light hatch
XHatchFill	8	Heavy cross hatch
InterleaveFill	9	Interleaving line
WideDotFill	10	Widely spaced dot
CloseDotFill	11	Closely spaced dot
UserFill	12	User-defined

SetFTime

Dos

Syntax

```
Procedure SetFTime( var F :
    AnyFileType; Time : LongInt );
```

Purpose

Sets the timestamp of an open file.

SetGraphBufSize

Graph

Syntax

```
Procedure SetGraphBufSize( BufSize :
    Word );
```

Purpose

Allocates BufSize bytes for the graphics buffer used for scan and flood fills. The default buffer size is 4K.

SetGraphMode

Graph

Syntax

```
Procedure SetGraphMode(Mode:Integer);
```

Purpose

Sets the system to the specified graphics Mode and clears the screen.

SetIntVec

Dos

Syntax

```
Procedure SetIntVec( IntNo : Byte;
Vector : Pointer );
```

Purpose

Sets interrupt vector `IntNo` to point to the address specified by `Vector`.

SetLineStyle

Graph

Syntax

```
Procedure SetLineStyle( LineStyle,
   Pattern, Thickness : Word );
```

Purpose

Sets the current `LineStyle`, `Pattern`, and `Thickness`. The `LineStyle` parameter controls the pattern of segments and spaces that actually form the line. Standard styles may be selected from among the following predefined constants:

Constant	
Name	*Value*
SolidLn	0
DottedLn	1
CenterLn	2
DashedLn	3
UserBitLn	4

If `UserBitLn` is chosen, then the line style takes the form of the sequence of bits within the `Pattern` byte; otherwise, the value of `Pattern` is ignored. The `Thickness` parameter chooses whether the line is normal or thick, depending upon the choice of the following predefined constants:

```
NormWidth  = 1;
ThickWidth = 3;
```

SetPalette

Graph

Syntax

```
Procedure SetPalette( ColorNum : Word;
    NewColor : ShortInt );
```

Purpose

Changes the setting of the ColorNum entry in the palette to NewColor.

SetRGBPalette

Graph

Syntax

```
Procedure SetRGBPalette( ColorNum,
    RedValue, GreenValue, BlueValue :
    Integer );
```

Purpose

Modifies the palette entry ColorNum for the IBM-8514 and VGA drivers.

The choice of ColorNum must be within the range allowed by the graphics driver: 0 through 255 for the IBM-8514, and 0 through 15 for the VGA. RedValue, GreenValue, and BlueValue allow user control of the intensities of the three color guns in the CRT. Typical colors are determined as follows:

Color	Red	Green	Blue
Black	$00	$00	$00
Blue	$00	$00	$FC
Green	$24	$FC	$24
Cyan	$00	$FC	$FC
Red	$FC	$14	$14
Magenta	$B0	$00	$FC

Color	Red	Green	Blue
Brown	$70	$48	$00
White	$C4	$C4	$C4
Gray	$34	$34	$34
Lt. Blue	$00	$00	$70
Lt. Green	$00	$70	$00
Lt. Cyan	$00	$70	$70
Lt. Red	$70	$00	$00
Lt. Magenta	$70	$00	$70
Yellow	$FC	$FC	$24
Bright White	$FC	$FC	$FC

SetTextBuf

System

Syntax

```
Procedure SetTextBuf( var F : Text;
    var Buf [; Size : Word ] );
```

Purpose

Assigns an I/O buffer of Buf to an unopened text file. If SetTextBuf is called and the optional Size parameter is specified, the buffer is set to the first Size bytes of Buf. If the Size parameter is omitted, the buffer size is assumed to be SizeOf(Buf) bytes.

SetTextJustify

Graph

Syntax

```
Procedure SetTextJustify( Horizontal,
    Vertical : Word );
```

Purpose

Sets the text justification for strings output by OutText and OutTextXY. The Horizontal parameter selects left, center, or right justification. Predefined constants are

```
LeftText   = 0;
CenterText = 1;
RightText  = 2;
```

The Vertical parameter selects bottom, center, or top justification. Predefined constants:

```
BottomText = 0;
CenterText = 1;
TopText    = 2;
```

SetTextStyle

Graph

Syntax

```
Procedure SetTextStyle( Font,
    Direction, Magnification : Word );
```

Purpose

Sets the current text Font, Direction, and character Magnification factor. Predefined constants for Font are

```
DefaultFont   = 0;    { GRAPH.TPU }
TriplexFont   = 1;    {  TRIP.CHR }
SmallFont     = 2;    {  LITT.CHR }
SansSerifFont = 3;    {  SANS.CHR }
GothicFont    = 4;    {  GOTH.CHR }
```

DefaultFont is the default 8×8 bit-mapped font. All others are stroked fonts.

Predefined constants for Direction are

```
HorizDir = 0;   { left to right }
VertDir  = 1;   { bottom to top }
```

SetTime

Syntax

```
Procedure SetTime( Hour, Minute,
    Second, Sec100 : Word );
```

Purpose

Sets the current time in the operating system.

SetUserCharSize

Syntax

```
Procedure SetUserCharSize( MultX,
    DivX, MultY, DivY : Word );
```

Purpose

Sets character width and height for stroked fonts. The horizontal factor is given by MultX div DivX, and the vertical factor by MultY div DivY.

SetVerify

Syntax

```
Procedure SetVerify(Verify: Boolean);
```

Purpose

Sets the state of the verify flag in DOS.

SetViewPort

Graph

Syntax

```
Procedure SetViewPort( X1, Y1, X2, Y2:
    Integer; Clip : Boolean);
```

Purpose

Sets the size and location of the window to use for graphics output. The upper left corner of the window is positioned at (X1, Y1), and the lower right corner at (X2, Y2).

SetVisualPage

Graph

Syntax

```
Procedure SetVisualPage(Page : Word);
```

Purpose

Selects video page. Multiple pages (page numbers other than 0) are supported only by EGA (256K), VGA, and Hercules graphics adapters; see SetActivePage for a list of valid drivers and modes. The SetVisualPage procedure will be ignored if it is executed when any other driver or mode is active.

SetWriteMode

Graph

Syntax

```
Procedure SetWriteMode( WriteMode :
    Integer );
```

Purpose

Sets the writing mode for line drawing. The `Write-Mode` parameter determines the binary operation used to place the line on the screen:

```
CopyPut = 0;    { MOV }
XORPut  = 1;    { XOR }
```

`CopyPut` uses an ordinary assembly language MOV instruction, overwriting the contents of the screen. `XORPut` uses an XOR instruction, which activates pixels when the screen is blank and deactivates pixels when the screen is lit.

Sin

System

Syntax

```
Function Sin( X : Real ) : Real;
```

Purpose

Returns the sine of the argument (in radians).

SizeOf

System

Syntax

```
Function SizeOf( X : AnyType ) : Word;
```

Purpose

Returns the number of bytes occupied by the argument, which can be any variable reference or type identifier.

Sound

Crt

Syntax
```
Procedure Sound( Hz : Word );
```

Purpose

Causes the internal speaker to generate a tone of Hz hertz (cycles per second). Typical settings for Hz include these, which constitute a musical scale:

	Frequency
Note	*(Hertz)*
C	523
D	587
E	659
F	699
G	784
A	880
B	988

The tone continues until turned off by NoSound.

SPtr

System

Syntax
```
Function SPtr : Word;
```

Purpose

Returns the current contents of the SP register.

Sqr

Syntax

```
Function Sqr( X : AnyType ) : AnyType;
```

Purpose

Returns the square of the argument, which can be any integer-type or real-type expression. The result is the same type as the argument.

Sqrt

Syntax

```
Function Sqrt( X : Real ) : Real;
```

Purpose

Returns the square root of the argument.

SSeg

Syntax

```
Function SSeg : Word;
```

Purpose

Returns the current value of the SS register.

Str

System

Syntax

```
Procedure Str( X [: Wid [: Decim] ];
    var S : String );
```

Purpose

Writes in S the string representation of the value X, which may be any integer-type or real-type expression.

Succ

System

Syntax

```
Function Succ( X : OrdType ) :
    OrdType;
```

Purpose

Returns the successor of the ordinal-type argument.

Swap

System

Syntax

```
Function Swap( X : IntWord ) :
    IntWord;
```

Purpose

Swaps the high- and low-order bytes of the argument, which can be either an Integer or a Word.

SwapVectors

Dos

Syntax

```
Procedure SwapVectors;
```

Purpose

Swaps interrupt vectors prior to a call to the Exec procedure.

TextBackground

Crt

Syntax

```
Procedure TextBackground(Color: Byte);
```

Purpose

Selects the background Color from one of the following predefined constants:

```
Black     = 0;
Blue      = 1;
Green     = 2;
Cyan      = 3;
Red       = 4;
Magenta   = 5;
Brown     = 6;
LightGray = 7;
```

TextColor

Crt

Syntax

```
Procedure TextColor( Color : Byte );
```

Purpose

Selects the foreground character `Color` from one of the following predefined constants:

```
Black        =  0;
Blue         =  1;
Green        =  2;
Cyan         =  3;
Red          =  4;
Magenta      =  5;
Brown        =  6;
LightGray    =  7;
DarkGray     =  8;
LightBlue    =  9;
LightGreen   = 10;
LightCyan    = 11;
LightRed     = 12;
LightMagenta = 13;
Yellow       = 14;
White        = 15;
```

A blinking effect can be achieved by adding the predefined constant Blink (128).

TextHeight

Graph

Syntax

```
Function TextHeight( TextString :
    String ) : Word;
```

Purpose

Returns the height of a string in pixels. The value is calculated from the current font size and multiplication factor.

TextMode

Crt

Syntax

```
Procedure TextMode( Mode : Integer );
```

Purpose

Selects a specific text Mode from the following list of predefined constants:

Constant Name	Value	Description
BW40	0	40×25 B/W on Color Adapter
CO40	1	40×25 Color on Color Adapter
BW80	2	80×25 B/W on Color Adapter
CO80	3	80×25 Color on Color Adapter
Mono	7	80×25 on Monochrome Adapter
Font8×8	256	Add-in for ROM font

TextWidth

Graph

Syntax

```
Function TextWidth( TextString :
    String ) : Word;
```

Purpose

Returns the width (in pixels) of a string.

Trunc

System

Syntax

```
Function Trunc( X : Real ) : LongInt;
```

Purpose

Truncates a real-type value to an integer-type value.

Truncate

System

Syntax

```
Procedure Truncate(var F:
    AnyFileType);
```

Purpose

Truncates file F by deleting all records beyond the
current file position.

UnpackTime

Dos

Syntax

```
Procedure UnpackTime( Time : LongInt;
    var Legible : DateTime );
```

Purpose

Converts the 4-byte, packed date-and-time longint
Time returned by GetFTime, FindFirst, or
FindNext into Legible, an unpacked DateTime
record.

UpCase

System

Syntax

```
Function UpCase( ch : Char ) : Char;
```

Purpose

Converts a character to uppercase.

Val

System

Syntax

```
Procedure Val( Orig : String;  var
    Final; var Code : Integer );
```

Purpose

Converts the original string value Orig to its numeric representation Final. If the string can't be converted, Code will contain the index of the first troublesome character. No trailing spaces are allowed.

WhereX

Crt

Syntax

```
Function WhereX : Byte;
```

Purpose

Returns the X-coordinate of the current cursor position, relative to the current window.

WhereY

Crt

Syntax

```
Function WhereY: Byte;
```

Purpose

Returns the Y-coordinate of the current cursor position, relative to the current window.

Window

Crt

Syntax

```
Procedure Window(X1,Y1,X2,Y2 : Byte);
```

Purpose

Defines a text window on the screen. The window is in the form of a rectangle, with upper left coordinates (X1, Y1) and lower right coordinates (X2, Y2).

Write

System

Syntax

```
Procedure Write( [var F : FileType;]
    v1 [ ,v2, ..., vn ] );
```

Purpose

Writes one or more values to a typed or text file. If the file identifier F is present and F is declared as a typed file, then each individual parameter v must be a variable of the same type as the component type of F.

If the file identifier F is present and F is declared as a text file, then each individual parameter v must be of type char, integer, real, string, or boolean. If the optional file identifier F is omitted, the destination is assumed to be the standard Output text file.

If the parameter is a boolean expression, one of the strings 'True' or 'False' will be written.

If output is to a text file, then each parameter v may have the form:

```
OutParam [ : MinWid [ : DecPlaces ] ]
```

where OutParam is an output expression. The optional fields MinWid and DecPlaces, if present, may be written as constants, variables, or expressions, but they must evaluate to integers.

MinWid is interpreted as the minimum desired width of the data item. If MinWid is larger than the data item, then the data item is right justified and given one or more leading spaces. On the other hand, if the data item is larger than MinWid, the compiler will automatically expand the width of the field; the data item will not be truncated. If MinWid is omitted, each output parameter is written using its default length, with a single additional space allowed for a plus or minus sign in front of each numeric value. Real numbers will be written out in scientific notation.

If the output parameter is a real number, then DecPlaces specifies the number of characters to follow the decimal point. If necessary, the compiler will automatically round the number.

Writeln

Syntax

```
Procedure Writeln( [var F : Text;] v1
   [ ,v2, ..., vn ] );
```

Purpose

Executes the `Write` procedure, then outputs an end-of-line marker to the file. If the optional text file identifier F is omitted, the standard `Output` file is assumed.

Predefined Data Structures

Predefined data structures and types are listed here in alphabetical order. The unit in which each structure or type is defined appears in a comment.

```
ArcCoordsType = record   { Graph }
   X, Y,
   Xstart, Ystart,
   Xend, Yend : Integer;
end;

DateTime = record { Dos }
   Year, Month, Day, Hour, Min, Sec : Word;
end;

DirStr  = String[67];    { Dos }

ExtStr  = String[4]; { Dos }

FillPatternType = { Graph }
   Array[1..8] of Byte;

FillSettingsType = record  { Graph }
   Pattern, Color : Word;
end;

LineSettingsType = record  { Graph }
   LineStyle, Pattern, Thickness : Word;
end;
```

```
NameStr = String[8]; { Dos }

PaletteType = record { Graph }
   Size : Byte;
   Colors : Array[0..MaxColors] of ShortInt;
end;

PathStr = String[79];    { Dos }

PointType = record    { Graph }
   X, Y : Integer;
end;

Registers = record    { Dos }
   Integer of
   0 : (AX,BX,CX,DX,BP,SI,DI,DS,ES,Flags :
   Word );
   1 : ( AL,AH,BL,BH,CL,CH,DL, DH : Byte );
end;

SearchRec = record    { Dos }
   Fill : Array[1..21] of Byte;
   Attr : Byte;
   Time, Size : LongInt;
   Name : String[12];
end;

TextSettingsType = record   { Graph }
   Font, Direction, CharSize, Horiz, Vert:
   Word;
end;

ViewPortType = record    { Graph }
   X1, Y1, X2, Y2 : Integer;
   Clip           : Boolean;
end;
```

Compiler Directives

There are three categories of directives: switch, parameter, and conditional. *Switch* directives, as their name implies, act to switch particular code-generation options on or off. *Parameter* directives specify external file names and memory sizes. *Conditional* directives are used to conditionally select which parts of a program are to be compiled and which parts are to be ignored.

Switch Directives

Switch directives allow you to choose from among several different code-generation options. Switch directives may be either *global*, meaning that the entire compilation is affected, or *local*, meaning that the option is in effect only until the next use of the same directive. In other words, once a global directive is set, it cannot be changed, while local directives can be switched on or off as often as needed. Global directives must be declared immediately after the initial `program` or `unit` heading line. Local directives may appear anywhere in the program.

Several switch directives can be specified within the same comment line by separating them with commas, as follows:

```
{$A+,B-,C+,... <any desired comment>}
```

A, B, and C may be any option. The + indicates that the option is enabled while the - indicates that the option is disabled. Any spaces appearing before the presence of a directive will cause the remainder of the line to be treated as a comment, and any additional directives will be ignored.

A: ALIGN DATA

Global

Syntax
    `{$A+}` or `{$A-}`

Default
    `{$A+}`

Menu
    Options/Compiler/Align Data

Purpose

The Align Data directive allows you to choose between
byte and word alignment when storing variables and
typed constants. The directive has no effect on the
functional operation of the program itself.

In the default state {$A+}, every variable and typed
constant requiring two or more bytes is stored in a
memory location that begins on an even address. When
word alignment is disabled with {$A-}, all data items
are stored continuously in memory, without any
consideration for their individual sizes or beginning
addresses.

B: BOOLEAN EVALUATION

Local

Syntax

{$B+} or {$B-}

Default

{$B-}

Menu

Options/Compiler/Boolean Evaluation

Purpose

The Boolean Evaluation directive allows the option of
evaluating a Boolean expression only as far as necessary to determine the result of the entire expression.

In the default state {$B-}, the compiler generates
code containing exits which allow the program to end
the Boolean evaluation after the result of the entire
expression becomes evident. This feature is commonly
known as "short circuit Boolean evaluation."

If the {$B+} option is enabled, the entire Boolean
expression is evaluated.

D: DEBUG INFORMATION

Global

Syntax

  {$D+} or {$D-}

Default

  {$D+}

Menu

  Options/**C**ompiler/**D**ebug Information

Purpose

  When the *Debug Information* option is enabled with
  {$D+}, the Turbo Pascal debugger can relate a
  program's source code to the machine code produced
  by the compiler. The *Debug Information* option is what
  allows the TURBO.EXE integrated development
  environment to respond to a run-time error by automatically returning to the editor and highlighting the
  offending source code.

  In addition, the *Debug Information* option provides the
  information needed for Turbo's built-in debugger to
  allow a program to run freely, to be "single-stepped,"
  or to run until a user-defined breakpoint is reached—all
  while displaying the effect of the program's statements.

E: EMULATION

Global

Syntax

  {$E+} or {$E-}

Default

  {$E+}

Menu

Options/Compiler/Emulation

Purpose

The 8087 Emulation directive controls whether floating-point emulation software is to be included with a compiled program.

In the default state {$E+}, the compiled program contains all the software necessary to emulate the operation of an 8087 coprocessor. The program may use any floating-point data types, including single, double, extended, and comp.

If 8087 emulation is disabled with {$E-}, the only software emulation that Turbo Pascal will include in the compiled program is code to support the 6-byte real data type. The program may still use the single, double, extended, and comp data types, but if it does, it can only run on a PC in which a math coprocessor has been installed, and the program must have been compiled with the {$N+} compiler directive enabled.

F: FORCE FAR CALLS

Local

Syntax

{$F+} or {$F-}

Default

{$F-}

Menu

Options/Compiler/Force Far Calls

Purpose

The Force Far Calls directive determines whether the

code generated for making procedure and function calls uses the near or far call model.

Far calls allow the program to reference a subroutine anywhere in memory. Both the segment and offset values must be specified; four bytes are required to contain the address. *Near* calls can only reference a subroutine within the current segment; only the two-byte offset is specified.

When the option is enabled with {$F+}, *all* calls use the far model.

I: INPUT/OUTPUT CHECKING

Local

Syntax
    {$I+} or {$I-}

Default
    {$I+}

Menu
    Options/Compiler/**I**/O Checking

Purpose

The I/O Checking directive controls whether code is generated to test for input and output errors.

When the option is enabled with {$I+}, the compiler automatically tests every I/O procedure and function. If any problem is detected, the program immediately terminates with a run-time error.

When the option is disabled with {$I-}, a single I/O error will suspend all further input and output activity, but won't cause program termination. In this case, I/O errors can be detected—and I/O processing restored—by calling the `IOResult` function. If `IOResult` returns zero, the operation was successful; a nonzero value corresponds to an error code that the program can use to determine an appropriate response. Note that when I/O Checking is disabled, the `IOResult` function *must* be called after every individual input and output statement.

L: LOCAL SYMBOL INFORMATION

Global

Syntax

    {$L+} or {$L-}

Default

    {$L+}

Menu

    Options/Compiler/Local Symbols

Purpose

The Local Symbol directive determines whether Local symbol information is included as part of the program's output.

When the Local Symbol option is enabled with {$L+}, the Turbo Pascal integrated debugger can access a program's local variables. In addition, the Debug/Call Stack menu option can be used to analyze the parameters passed in procedure and function calls.

The Local Symbol directive is usually enabled in conjunction with the Debug Information directive {$D+}. The Local Symbol option allows the debugger to track individual local symbols, while the Debug Information option can relate those symbols to specific lines of program code.

N: NUMERIC PROCESSING

Global

Syntax

{$N+} or {$N-}

Default

{$N-}

Menu

Options/Compiler/Numeric Processing

Purpose

The Numeric Processing directive determines whether an installed 8087 coprocessor will be used to handle floating-point operations.

By default, the Numeric Processing option is disabled. The program will execute just as if no 8087 is present— regardless of the actual configuration of the PC.

In the {$N+} state, the compiler will try to use the coprocessor whenever it encounters an instruction involving an operation on one or more real numbers. If no coprocessor is present, emulation software may be invoked, depending upon the setting of the {$E} 8087 Emulation option.

O: OVERLAY CODE GENERATION

Global

Syntax

{$O+} or {$O-}

Default

{$O-}

Menu

Options/Compiler/Overlays Allowed

Purpose

The Overlay Code Generation directive enables or disables the generation of the special code that allows a unit to be used as an overlay. This code consists of slightly different parameter-passing routines, which—while not as efficient as the default routines—nevertheless have the same functionality. Hence, the use of the {$O+} directive doesn't *force* the unit to be used as an overlay; it simply tells the compiler that the unit *can* be used as an overlay.

R: RANGE CHECKING

Local

Syntax

{$R+} or {$R-}

Default

{$R-}

Menu

Options/Compiler/Range Checking

Purpose

The Range Checking option enables or disables the generation of code designed to perform range-checking (for array indexes, enumerated types, etc.) in an executing program.

When the Range Checking option is enabled with {$R+}, Turbo Pascal will generate code to ensure that each reference to the subscript of an array or string is within the defined bounds of the variable. In addition, the compiler will ensure that each assignment to a scalar or subrange variable is within the appropriate range. If the range-checking code detects any out-of-bounds condition, the program will terminate with a run-time error.

S: STACK OVERFLOW CHECKING

Local

Syntax
    {$S+} or {$S-}

Default
    {$S+}

Menu
Options/Compiler/Stack Checking

Purpose
The Stack Overflow Checking directive enables or disables the generation of code to check whether a stack overflow condition is encountered. In the default state, when the Stack Overflow Checking option is enabled, the compiler generates code to calculate—*prior* to a function or procedure call—whether there is sufficient stack space remaining to contain both the passed parameters and any local variables.

V: VAR-STRING CHECKING

Local

Syntax
    {$V+} or {$V-}

Default
    {$V+}

Menu
Options/**C**ompiler/**V**ar-String Checking

Purpose
The Var-String Checking directive determines whether
or not strict type-checking is performed on strings
passed as variable parameters to functions and procedures.

In the default state {$V+}, formal and actual string
parameters must be the same type. When the option is
disabled, a subroutine will accept strings of any size.

Although strong-typing helps to ensure that variables
are properly used, disabling Var-String Checking
allows you to develop generic string routines.

Parameter Directives

While a procedure or function parameter serves to pass
information to a subroutine, a program parameter
passes information to the operating system. Program
parameters are principally concerned with file names
and DOS memory allocation requirements.

I: INCLUDE FILE

Local

Syntax
    {$I filename}

Menu
Options/**D**irectories/**I**nclude Directories

Purpose

The Include File directive instructs the compiler to insert the contents of the named file immediately after the occurrence of the directive. The directive may appear anywhere in your program, except that it cannot be located within a `begin...end` statement block.

The default file name extension is .PAS. A directory may be specified. If the file isn't found, the compiler will search the directories named in the **O**ptions/ **D**irectories/**I**nclude Directories menu.

Include files may be nested up to eight levels deep.

L: LINK OBJECT FILE

Local

Syntax

    {$L filename}

Menu

Options/**D**irectories/**O**bject Directories

Purpose

The Link Object File directive identifies a file to be linked with the program or unit currently being compiled. Files to be linked must be in proper Intel relocatable object file (.OBJ) format.

The default file name extension is .OBJ. A directory may be specified. If the file isn't found, the compiler will search the directories named in the **O**ptions/ **D**irectories/**O**bject Directories menu.

M: MEMORY ALLOCATION SIZES

Global

Syntax

    {$M stacksize, heapmin, heapmax}

Default

    {$M 16384, 0, 655360}

Menu

Options/Compiler/Memory Sizes

Purpose

The Memory Allocation directive specifies the amount of memory to be allocated for the program's stack and heap.

Default, minimum, and maximum sizes are shown below. Only integer values are accepted.

	Default	*Minimum*	*Maximum*
stacksize	16,384	1,024	65,520
heapmin	0	0	655,360
heapmax	655,360	heapmin	655,360

The Memory Allocation directive is global. It can only appear within the main module; the option is ignored when included in a unit.

O: OVERLAY UNIT NAME

Local

Syntax

    {$O unitname}

Menu

None

Purpose

The Overlay Unit Name directive tells the compiler which external units are to be converted into overlays (.OVR files) rather than be included in the current executable (.EXE) file.

The directive must appear after the `unitname` is referenced by the `uses` clause. If the directive appears within a unit, or if it references the System unit, it will be ignored.

Conditional Compilation Directives

Conditional compilation allows separate sections of a single program to be compiled, based entirely on user-defined conditions. This feature is particularly useful for debugging large programs and for tailoring a general program to fit a variety of specific applications or installations.

The conditionally compiled portions of code are placed within logical block structures, which are entirely independent of any program logic. The basic format of a conditional compilation block is:

`{$IFxxx }`	The `$IFxxx` statement tests a condition.
`....`	These statements are compiled only if
`....`	the condition in the `$IFxxx` statement is True.
`{$ELSE}`	The optional `$ELSE` designates alternate code.
`....`	These statements are compiled only if
`....`	the condition in the `$IFxxx` statement is False.
`{$ENDIF}`	One `$ENDIF` is required for each `$IF` block.

Any legal Pascal statement may appear within a conditional compilation block, including directives, data, and program code. The {$IFxxx} statements may be nested up to 16 levels deep, but each must be terminated with an {$ENDIF} statement. Whenever an {$ELSE} appears, it always refers to the most recently defined {$IFxxx}. If conditional compilation statements are used within an include file, you must ensure that each file has balanced pairs of {$IFxxx} and {$ENDIF} statements.

The {$IFDEF} and {$IFNDEF} statements evaluate symbols defined by other conditional compilation statements or predefined within Turbo Pascal. Symbols are defined and undefined (that is, set to True and False) with the directives:

```
{$DEFINE SymbolName}
{$UNDEF SymbolName}
```

The {$UNDEF} directive cancels a previous definition; if SymbolName hadn't been previously defined, it would have automatically evaluated to False.

The predefined conditional symbols are listed in the following table.

Symbols	Defined (True) When
VER40	The current compiler version is 4.0
VER50	The current compiler version is 5.0
MSDOS	The current operating system is MS-DOS
CPU86	The CPU is an Intel 80×86 processor
CPU87	An 80×87 coprocessor is present

DEFINE

Syntax

```
{$DEFINE name}
```

Purpose

The DEFINE directive both defines a conditional symbol for use by other directives and sets the symbol to Boolean True. If `name` has already been defined, the directive is ignored.

UNDEF

Syntax

`{$UNDEF name}`

Purpose

The UNDEF directive removes the definition of a conditional symbol. In effect, the symbol is set to Boolean False. If `name` has already been undefined, the directive is ignored.

IFDEF

Syntax

`{$IFDEF name}`

Purpose

The IFDEF directive compiles the following section of code if the conditional symbol `name` has been defined in a DEFINE directive.

IFNDEF

Syntax

`{$IFNDEF name}`

Purpose

The IFNDEF directive compiles the following section of code if the conditional symbol `name` has not been defined with a DEFINE directive or if `name` has been undefined with an UNDEF directive.

IFOPT

Syntax

```
{$IFOPT switch}
```

Purpose

The `{IFOPT switch}` directive compiles the following section of code if the switch is enabled or disabled, as indicated. For example, if a program contained the directives for enabling numeric processing, it could additionally allow 8087 emulation to be disabled as follows:

```
{$IFOPT N+}
{$E-}
{$ENDIF}
```

ELSE

Syntax

```
{$ELSE}
```

Purpose

The ELSE directive compiles the following section of code if the most recent `IFxxx` is not True.

ENDIF

Syntax

{$ENDIF}

Purpose

The ENDIF directive marks the end of the most recent IFxxx or ELSE section.

Index